New Nightingale, New Rose

New Nightingale, New Rose

Poems from the Divan of Hafiz

Translated by Richard Le Gallienne
Introduction by Andrew Phillip Smith

Bardic Press
California
2004

Copyright © Bardic Press 2004
Introduction Copyright © Andrew Phillip Smith 2004
Cover Design by Roosje Penfold
Printed on acid-free paper
Originally published as
Odes From the Divan of Hafiz, Boston, 1903

Published by Bardic Press
PO Box 761
Oregon House
CA 95962
USA
http://www.Bardic-Press.com

Hafiz, 14th cent.
[Divan. English. Selections]
New Nightingale, New Rose\Poems from the Divan of Hafiz
p. cm.
ISBN 0-9745667-0-5
Sufi poetry, Persian—Translations into English.
I.Le Gallienne, Richard. II. Title.
PK6465.Z31 H34 2004
891'.5511—dc21 2003113817
Library of Congress Control Number 2003113817

Contents

Introduction by Andrew Phillip Smith   i
Poems from the Divan of Hafiz   1
Glossary   161

Introduction

Nightingale, have you heard the news!
The Rose has come back and the green and the blue,
And everything is as new as the dew—
New nightingale, new rose.

For well over two hundred years the poetry of Hafiz has been appearing in English translation. The very first of these was the Persian Song in 1771, a baroque translation of the eighth poem in the Divan, by William Jones. Others followed and by now over a hundred different translators have tried their hands at Hafiz. The most notable recent translations are the very popular, very modern and exceedingly free versions of Daniel Ladinsky. Halfway between these two, published a century before the writing of this preface, Richard Le Gallienne produced a translation of one hundred of Hafiz's poems. First published in New York in 1903, the poems went into several reprintings over the next twenty years, and must be counted among the most popular translations of Hafiz.

Richard Le Gallienne was one of the decadent poets, a member of the Rhymers Club that met in the Cheshire Cheese pub off Fleet Street in the 1890s. He was thus a contemporary and associate of such characters as W. B. Yeats, Oscar Wilde, Ernest Dowson, and Aubrey Beardsley, to name only a few. This was an age of exquisite lyrics and most of the poets of this time had a fine control over the musicality of English verse. Yeats dubbed the poets of the 1890s 'the tragic generation', since so many of them had died early deaths and lived life with a hopeless recklessness. This poignancy comes through in these translations of Hafiz, but Le Gallienne must have been a little healthier and more stable, or just luckier, than the others, since he outlived them all. His only daughter, Eva Le Gallienne, became a well-known actress.

The novelist Llewelyn Powys wrote, "Of all the poets I know, I think Richard Le Gallienne looks most like a poet... Richard Le Gallienne always represented to my mind the last of the great figures of the Nineties; and in truth, because of a certain look of fatality he wore over his shoulders, like Caesar's cloak, one was constantly being reminded that one was talking with a man who had sat at meat with Swinburne, with Downson, with Lionel Johnson, and with Oscar Wilde."

Le Gallienne was born in Liverpool in 1866. He moved to London where he became a professional litterateur—an editor, writer and poet. Previous to his Hafiz translations he had produced a superb, pithy, direct translation of the Rubaiyat of Omar Khayyam (also available soon from Bardic Press.) His translations of Hafiz are what would now be called versions or renderings, and what were then called paraphrases. Le Gallienne can often be very free with Hafiz's originals, but the end result is a translation that is poetry in English. While there are many more literal translations, Le Gallienne's has a depth of feeling, a felicity and musicality that is unsurpassed even by Gertrude Bell's translations. Yeats included A Caravan from China Comes in his controversial Oxford Book of Modern Verse, and the scholar A.J.Arberry included a number of Le Gallienne's translations in his anthology Fifty Poems of Hafiz. Selections were even set to music by W. Franke Harling in 1913 and by Elliot Griffis in 1920.

Le Gallienne's Hafiz is a muse-inspired love poet, a poet of Spring, and a great drinker. His Hafiz reminds us of the Chinese Li Po and the Welsh Dafydd ap Gwilym, though Le Gallienne may never have read either of them. Although Hafiz is now seen in the West as a mystical poet in the Sufi tradition, there was previously a good deal of scholarly controversy over the Sufi content of Hafiz's works. Le Gallienne takes the view that Hafiz is, for the most part, writing of real wine and real women, and so he translates accordingly. "Whatever mystical meanings may lie beneath, on the surface, at all events, the poems of Hafiz seem easy to understand, and if they should have a secondary significance, most of us will, I think, be content to take them in their primary aspect as lyrical expressions of the joy and sorrow of earth." Yet Le Gallienne's Hafiz can still gaze beyond his mortal beloved to an immortal Beloved, and his intoxification is not only literal:

> Hafiz is drunk in many different ways—
> Drunk with the Infinite, Drunk with the divine,
> With music drunk, and many a lovely face;
> Also, he's drunk—with wine.

We might compare Hafiz's ghazels to the Song of Solomon, or to Shakespeare's sonnets, or to Dante's Vita Nuova. All of these have an inner meaning, but if we ignore the romantic love expressed in them, and take them only in an intellectually symbolic way, we miss the poetry. Surely a man who writes so much of women and wine was very fond of both, and the emotions aroused by romantic love can be transformed into those of divine love. One of Hafiz's patrons, Shah Shuja, complained that Hafiz's verse "was at one moment mystical, at another erotic and bacchanalian, now serious and spiritual, and again flippant and worldly, or worse."

Sufis come in for a certain amount of criticism in Le Gallienne's translations. If we substitute 'priest' or 'monk' here, we will get the idea; when Le Gallienne mentions Sufis, he usually means those people who give themselves to external piety. Yet Hafiz himself, and not just Richard Le Gallienne, can regard Sufis as needlessly austere, as in ghazals 329 or 492, not represented in this collection. There are Sufis and there are Sufis.

Hafiz was born around 1320AD in Shiraz, Persia. He was a contemporary of other fourteenth century notables such as Chaucer and Petrarch and, in the Islamic world, of the infamous conqueror Tamerlane, and of the poets Ibn-I-Yamin and Salman-I-Sawaji. Hafiz is a title for someone who has memorised the entire Koran: the poet's given name was Shams-ud-din Mohammed. Hafiz lived in a time of political commotion, of coups and upheavals, though Shiraz escaped the worst results of the invasions of the Mongols and the Tartars. His father died when he was relatively young and he had two older brothers; between the three of them they supported the family. Hafiz was bright, yet he had to work first for a draper and then at a bakery to help support the family. He is said to have written his first poem by completing a poem begun by his untalented uncle.

While there is little in the way of hard historical fact, a number of anecdotes are told of Hafiz, many of them with a legendary or symbolic quality. The most famous of them is as follows. When he was twenty-one, and working as a baker, Hafiz was delivering bread in a prosperous district of Shiraz. While doing his deliveries, he saw a beautiful woman and, of course, fell hopelessly in love with her. He was not a physically attractive man, nor, as a baker's boy, wealthy, and had little chance of successfully wooing her. Hafiz began to write poems about her, and the poems circulated and became popular in Shiraz. He was still as hopelessly in love with her as before but, even though she knew of his poetry, the love was unrequited.

There are a number of different versions of this story. According to the most developed version, Hafiz knew of a legend that told that anyone who could spend forty nights without sleep at the tomb of Baba Kuhi, a saint who died centuries earlier, would be granted his heart's desire. (A similar legend in Wales tells that whoever spends a night alone in certain places will the next morning be found dead, mad or will become a poet; the forty nights also reminds us of Jesus's forty days and nights in the wilderness, and of Moses's forty years in the desert.) Hafiz decided to keep this forty night sleepless vigil, even though, as a man who lived in the world, he had to work for the bakery during the day. He went to the tomb night after night, and by the end of the forty nights he was almost walking in his sleep. On the very last night, Shakh-I-Nabat, "the branch of sugarcane", the woman with whom Hafiz had fallen in love and for whom he was keeping this vigil, came to him as he was on his way to the saint's tomb, and declared her love for him, impressed as she was by his poems written of her, and his persistence. But Hafiz could only think of completing his vigil and staggered towards the tomb to spend his last sleepless night there.

At dawn the next day, the angel Gabriel appeared and asked Hafiz what his heart's desire was. Instead of telling

Gabriel that he wished his beloved Shakh-I-Nabat, he declared that, since God's angel, Gabriel, was so beautiful, then God must be even more beautiful. Hafiz exclaimed, "I wish God." Gabriel then directed Hafiz to a small grocery store where he would find a man named Attar, who became his teacher. Attar taught Hafiz for the next forty years. (Incidentally, this is not the same Attar as the famous, and earlier, author of the Conference of the Birds.)

Hafiz married and had at least one son, but it is not clear whether he married Shakh-I-Nabat or another woman. His poems became widely known, and he taught the Koran and became a court poet to Abou Ishak, the governor of Shiraz. Abou Ishak (who appears in poem 174) loved wine, poetry and pleasure so much that he neglected government and soon lost his kingdom to Mubariz Muzaffar. The capture of Shiraz by Mubariz Muzaffar resulted in Hafiz losing both of his positions. Muzaffar was a Sunni puritan who ordered the wine taverns to be closed: "It is a wonderful and wicked thing They at this season should the tavern close; Drink shall we none the less—under the rose; The Water of Life runs from this little spring." Yet another coup followed and Hafiz regained his position again when Muzaffar's son, Shah Shuja, overthrew his father. Shah Shuja reopened the taverns. This was the time when Hafiz was most prolific in his writing, but after a few years, he fell out of favour with his new master, and went in exile to Isfahan. He was allowed to return four years later.

Hafiz's wife and son both died within his lifetime, his son seemingly in childhood. He wife is thought to be commemorated in poems 227 and 598, his son in poem 606. Hafiz was Attar's pupil all this time, even though he was separated from him by exile. According to the story, when he was sixty years old Hafiz became tired of his forty year discipleship, and tired of waiting for union with God. In a move that echoes his forty night vigil, he drew a circle on the ground and stayed within it for forty days. At the end of this period, Gabriel appeared again to him, and asked him what he wished. By this time, Hafiz could only say that he wished to serve his teacher. He then returned to Attar's house, and his teacher greeted him with a cup of old wine. On drinking it

Hafiz finally attained union with God.

In one of the great crossings of history (or legend), Hafiz met Tamerlane, the bloody conqueror celebrated in Marlowe's Tamburlaine plays. It is a moment that reminds us of Alexander the Great sparing the house in Thebes where Pindar had lived, or of Goethe's meeting with Napoleon. In one of his most famous poems, Hafiz had written to his beloved, "I'll give to you Bokhara—yes! and Samarkand. Indeed, I'd give them for the mole upon your cheek." Tamerlane came from Samarkand and had conquered both cities. He asked Hafiz why he would give up these great cities for the mole on the cheek of a woman from Shiraz-wasn't this an insult to the conqueror? Hafiz, who was poor and had been unable to pay the tax demanded by Tamerlane's forces, replied, "It is because of such generosity that I find myself in such poverty!"

Hafiz died in 1389, and his tomb is in the garden of Musalla, through which the stream Rukbnabad flows. Both are celebrated in his poetry, and both are now famous because of him.

> For Ruknabad shall run and run,
> And each year, punctual as Spring,
> The new-born nightingale shall sing
> Unto Musella's new-born rose;
> But we shall not know anything,
> Nor laugh, nor weep, nor anywise
> Listen or speak, fast closed our eyes
> And shut our ears—in Paradise!

New Nightingale, New Rose

Poems from the Divan of Hafiz

1

Saki, for God's love, come and fill my glass;
    Wine for a breaking heart, O Saki, bring!
For this strange love which seemed at first, alas!
    So simple and so innocent a thing,
How difficult, how difficult it is!
        Because the night-wind kissed the scented curl
        On the white brow of a capricious girl,
And, passing, gave me half the stolen kiss,
    Who would have thought one's heart could bleed and break
For such a very little thing as this?
    Wine, Saki, wine—red wine, for pity's sake!

O Saki, would to God that I might die!
    Would that this moment I might hear the bell
        That bids the traveller for the road prepare,
    Be the next stopping-place or heaven or hell!
Strange caravan of death—no fears have I
        Of the dark journey, gladly would I dare
The fearful river and the whirling pools;
    Ah! they that dwell upon the other side,
        What know they of the burdens that we bear?
    With lit-up happy faces having died,
        What know they of Love's bitter mystery,
        The love that makes so sad a fool of me?
A fool of HAFIZ!—yea, a fool of fools.

2

O love, the beauty of the moon is thine,
And on thy chin a little star doth shine,
The jewel-dimple of thy little chin;
O how my soul desires the sight of thee,
And rushes to the windows of my eyes,
And to and fro about my body flies,
Half out of doors and half constrained within;
Ears all atremble for some word of thine,
Tongue tip-toe on the threshold of the lip,
And my full heart is like a stormy sea.

If only thou wouldst scatter on the breeze
A handful of the roses of thy cheek,
The faithful breeze would bring them safe to me;
Thy garden would not miss them from its trees,
And I would seem a little nearer thee—
Rose-garden of the neighbourhood of thee.

O lips of sugar, would that it were mine
Upon those paradisal lips to feed!—
Hark! the presumptuous fellow, how he sings!—
HAFIZ—how canst thou hope that she will heed,
And say Amen to such a prayer as thine?
Such lips are the predestined food of Kings.

7

Heart, have you heard the news!
    The Spring has come back—have you heard!
    With little green shoot and little pink bud, and the
        little new-hatched bird,
And the Rose—yes! yes! the Rose—
Nightingale, have you heard the news!
    The Rose has come back and the green and the blue,
    And everything is as new as the dew—
        New nightingale, new rose.

Wind of the east, flower-footed breeze,
O take my love to the budding trees,
    To the cypress take it, and take it, too,
To the tender nurslings of meadows and leas,
To the basil take it, messenger breeze,
    And I send it, my love, to you.

So glad am I of the new-found sun,
    I believe I could kiss the tavern door;
    Why, I could sweep the tavern floor
With the lashes of my eyes!

        O April skies!
        The Winter's done,
        O April skies!
        The Spring's begun;
        And honey-humming
        Summer's coming
        Close behind;
        O April skies!
        Even the tavern girl is kind.

HAFIZ, remember well how short is Spring,
    And drain the good days deep ere they depart
Thou nightingale that shall forever sing,
    Rose of thine own imperishable art!

2

Brothers, attend
How you shall spend
This fleeting treasure
Of days that pass:
Fill you your measure
With present pleasure,
The deep sweet glass,
And love and leisure,
And sunny grass.

Let the pious thunder
Of heaven and hell—
He drinks as well;
Let the proud man rear
His lofty towers—
Have you no fear;
The little flowers
That grow thereunder
Shall last as long—
Or a little song.

Not our Most High Lord
The Sultan's sword
Can more command,
When he comes to die,
Than you and I
Of simple birth
Can ask of earth—
A little land
In which to lie.

And, even now,
Who more would ask
Than just to bask
The blue sky under:
A little grass,
Wine in the glass,
One's liberty
And Love and wonder:
This, HAFIZ, is
Felicity.

8

You little Turk of Shiraz-Town,
    Freebooter of the hearts of men,
As beautiful, as says renown,
    Are your freebooting Turkomen;
Dear Turko-maid—a plunderer too—
    Here is my heart, and there your hand:
If you'll exchange, I'll give to you
    Bokhara—yes! and Samarkand.
    Indeed, I'd give them for the mole
Upon your cheek, and add thereto
    Even my body and my soul.

Come, bearer of the shining cup,
    Bring the red grape into the sun,
That we may drink, and drink it up,
    Before our little day is done;
    For Ruknabad shall run and run,
And each year, punctual as Spring,
The new-born nightingale shall sing
Unto Musella's new-born rose;
But we shall not know anything,
Nor laugh, nor weep, nor anywise
Listen or speak, fast closed our eyes
And shut our ears—in Paradise!

You little robber-woman, you
    Who turns the heads of Shiraz-Town,
With sugar-talk and sugar-walk
    And all your little sugar-ways,—
Into the sweet-shop of your eyes
    I innocently gaze and gaze,
    While, like your brethren of renown,
O little Turk of Shiraz, you
Plunder me of my patience too.

Yet all too well the lover knows
    The loved one needs no lover's praise;
What other perfume needs the rose?
Perfection needs no word of ours,
    Nor heeds what any song-bird says—
Sufficient unto flowers are flowers.

Nay, give it up! Nor try to probe
    Secret of her, or any heaven;
It is a most distracting globe—
    Seven the stars, our sins are seven;
Above no answer, nor below:
Let's call the Saki—he may know;
Yes, who knows, HE may know.

O love, that was not very kind!
    That answer that you gave to me;
Nay, I mistook, you spoke me well!
    For you to speak at all to me
    Is unforeseen felicity;
Yes, bitter on your lips grows sweet,
    And soft your hardest words to me.

Sweetheart, if you would hearken me,
    I am a very wise old thing,
And it were wise for you to hear.

My little Turk, my cypress dear,
    So wise this wisdom that I sing,
That some day on a shining string
High up in heaven, tear by tear,
    As star by star, these songs shall hang
At evening on the vestal sky,
    These little songs that Hafiz sang
    To one that heard not on his knees:
So well I sang them—even I—
    That, listening to them, Heaven's Lord
    Tossed me from heaven as reward
    The small change of the Pleiades!—
These little songs that Hafiz sang
To one that heard not on his knees.

9

O love, if thou so cruel continuest to be,
Like other fool fanatics to the wilderness I'll flee,
    And live on roots, religious-mad, up in the lonely
        mountains;
My head turned with religion, the Religion, love, of Thee.

Wind of the East, to my gazelle I beg thee go and say:
Remember him who beats the air like a madman night
    and day,
    A wild man in the desert drear, far from the pleasant
        fountains,
As bleak and homeless in his heart as the wind upon his
    way.

Ah! little sugar-seller, dost thou never one thought send
To this parrot of all eloquence, thy sugar-eating friend,
    Or is the rose too deep in love with her own face and
        fashion,
A frenzied nightingale to heed, or to his song attend?

It is goodness, O thou foolish-wise, and constancy, I heard,
Not trick and snare, that should attract the philosophic
    bird;
    But no such reasons can I give for my own fatal
        passion—
By every heartless wile and lure has HAFIZ been en-
    snared.

How strange it is these moons of girls, slim as the cypress-
    tree,
So lovely and so pitiless and so untrue should be!

    Ah! my own love, nought was left out from thine own
        finished fairness,
The little gift of being true—that only was denied thee.

HAFIZ, though she care not to hear—listen! what carest
        thou!
Zuhrah is singing there in heaven to god and goddess
        even now—
    So sweet she sings, and O the songs they are of such a
        rareness,
Messiah's self is dancing as she singeth them, I vow.

14

O love, how can you thus conceal your face,
    Hiding it thus each lost and listening day,
And, like the moon, blessing some other place,
    Leaving us watchers with no single ray
Of all that firmament that is your face;
O Lady, take some pity on our case,
    Nor leave unfed our hollow starving eyes;
Shower some silver from your hidden moon
    On us poor mendicants of Paradise:—

(Would, love, that I had never seen your face!
And yet—if I had never seen your face!)

    For, like the angel Harut, we are torn
    With love, from morn to midnight, back to morn,
With love so burning of your sacred face
    That often we grow angry we were born.

Yea! though so deep the pit and fierce with fire
    Where Harut stands, there is within thy chin
    A dimple-pit that I am standing in,—
A pit of wasting, white unslaked desire,—
    To which the burning Babylonian sands
    Where the great love-inflicted angel stands,
Burning immortally in body and soul,
Is cool as waters lapping round the pole.

O Hell within the heaven of your face!

O Love, the very perfume of the rose,
    As the dew carries it about the sward,
    Smiting my senses like an unseen sword,
Out from the rose-bush of your bosom blows;
    And lo! the very nightingales are mad,
    Frenzied with singing—just as though they had
Looked one delirious moment in your face.

O idol, do not stay too long away,
    Unless you would indeed your HAFIZ kill;
Scatter the clouds of absence; do not slay
    A heart so loving and so faithful still;
Be good to HAFIZ—bring him back your face.

16

"Love," I cried, "a little pity
Show to me, a hapless stranger,
Poor and lonely in Love's City."
But she answered: "Foolish stranger,
Yours the fault, not mine, for losing
Thus your way; it is your own choosing—
Blame not me, O tiresome stranger."

"Stay a little—don't refuse me;
Do so much for a poor stranger."
"Nay," she answered, "please excuse me."
All in vain I tried to change her;
How should she on ermine sleeping
Pay attention to the weeping
Of a lorn and outcast stranger;
What though stones should be his pillow,
And his couch of thorns—poor stranger!
She cares nothing for the fellow,
Delicately out of danger.

'Mid your curls and your caresses
Lost lie all our hearts—how strange
Is the network of your tresses!
And that little mole—how strange!
Down your cheek, like Chinese writing,
Steals the dusky down—how strange,
How adorably inviting!
Like a string of ants—how strange
Its soft shadow on the brightness
Of your moon cheek's milky whiteness,
Very white—and very strange;
White—yet just a little flushing

With the daintiest carmine;
Very delicately blushing,
Like a white rose dipped in wine.

Cruel love, I give you warning;
What if Heaven should hear the stranger,
And fulfil his prayers some morning,
Punish you—for this poor stranger;
Knowing well how you denied him
Food and shelter—woe betide him—
Sent away the starving stranger.
Night is falling, black and lonely,
Long and black as your long hair;
Where shall lodge the wretched stranger!
Sweetheart, just for this night only,
'Neath that star-lit tent of hair
Grant a lodging to a stranger.

All in vain I strive to change her,
HAFIZ, all in vain your prayer;
Can you wonder, you poor stranger!
All the world's in love with her.

17

Comrades, the morning breaks, the sun is up;
    Over her pearly shoulder the shy dawn
    Winds the soft floating mists of silver lawn;
Comrades, the morning cup! the morning cup!

With dew the tulip's cheek is dappled grey,
    And from the ground sweet smells of morning rise,
    The breeze blow softly out of Paradise;
Drink to the morning of another day!

The red rose sits upon her emerald throne,
    The glittering grass about her feet is spread;
    Wine, Saki, bright as fire, as rubies red!
Comrades, the morning cup, ere morn be flown!

What! they have shut the wine-house up again!
    On such a morning closed the tavern door!
    Great Opener of Doors, Thee we implore
Open it for us, for we knock in vain.

It is a wonderful and wicked thing
    They at this season should the tavern close;
    Drink shall we none the less—under the rose;
The Water of Life runs from this little spring.

Sikandar's mirror is this magic cup;
    In it the whole round world reflected lies;
    It is filled with pictures for anointed eyes;
It is the World's wisdom thou art drinking up.

Under the red rose drinking the red wine,
 In a red dawn, and kissing her red lips,
 No honey-bee from such a flower sips—
No emperor lives such a life as mine.

Once more, O HAFIZ, dawns the morning cup,
 Another day in which to seek her face!
 Patience! the day will come, in some strange place,
When thy strong hands her veil at last lift up.

24

Do you see that dark girl yonder?
    Black as Erebus her hair—
All the sweetness and the wonder
    Of the world belong to her:
Did you ever see a woman
    Quite so black—yet quite so fair?
Every goodness that is human
    Or divine belongs to her.
On her lips is all the wisdom,
    Sealed up with a ruby there—
Solomon's own seal and wisdom
    Both alike belong to her.
Golden is her skin, as golden
    As the wheat that proved a snare
To old Adam once in Eden—
    Yes, the Fall belongs to her:
Adam-like, I too have eaten,
    Adam-like is my despair—
Eaten the forbidden wheaten
    Whiteness that belongs to her.

On a journey she is starting,
    How can I the anguish bear!
O the pain of her departing!
    May the peace belong to her.
Yet if only she were feeling
    Just a little sorrier!
Wounded heart, your wound's past healing
    Healing too belongs to her.

Undefiled her skirt was ever
    By life's muddy thoroughfare,
Pure in sight of both worlds—never
    Breath of shame belongs to her.

Surely this is mystifying—
    I am dying of despair,
And that dark girl sees me dying;
    Yet she knows belongs to her
The holy breath revivifying
    Of Jesus Lord that Mary bare.

Yet if truly I must leave her,
    Even in the sepulchre,
HAFIZ, dying true believer,
    Still shall sing his songs to her.

26

Thrice holy night! O hallowed rising moon!
    O waiting trees! O stars that burn so bright!
O radiant planet, was it yours the boon?
This is the night of my first wondering look
    Into her eyes, the night she came to me
Right out of heaven—like the holy book;
    O bright beginning of felicity,
        This is the night.

Tonight the Mussulman is at his prayers;
    Spinning in solemn fury circle-wise,
The dervish chants; for holy church declares
    The Koran like a star shot from the skies—
        This very night.

I also shall observe the sacred rites:
    Bent low before her on adoring knees,
In a strong circle of my faithful love
    'I'll keep her safe as gold in sanctuaries.
O river singing to the stars above!
        O Night of Nights!

So beautiful the face of her I love,
    Heaven, like a proud and eager tiring-maid,
Holds up the moon as mirror for her gaze;
    And O when all her beauty is arrayed,
    She is a being so exceeding bright,
Even the burnished sun, with morn ablaze,
Shows like mere dust beneath her courser's feet—
    Yea! all her body is so filled with light.

In her all living brightness is complete,
    Bounded in her, as in some blinding sphere;
    And to the sun himself, till she appear,
        Day is as night.

Ah! Sufi, can you dream I will give up
    A love like this—for pious platitude,
Or cease to crush the grape into the cup!
    I, Sufi, may be wrong, you may be right—
HAFIZ must tread his self-appointed way
    And on her red lips find his heavenly food.
If you must talk, O talk some other day—
        But not tonight.

32

It is an unstable world: all fades and glides
And surely melts and vanishes away;
Even as the hollow wind we come and go,
Like the obliterating ebb and flow
Of wreck-encumbered shingle-shifting tides,
Forgotten as the iridescent spray.
Hope is a fairy palace built on sand,
And life's own tree is rooted in the wind;
Only this friend I hold here in my hand,
When all the rest have gone, remains behind—
Only the cup abides.

Saki, the servant of that man am I
Who kneels to nobody beneath the blue,
But, firm in spirit, lets the world go by.
Come, fill the cup—I have strange news for you!
How shall I utter what last night befell
Here in this reeking tavern unto me,
Drunk and adream and foolish with old wine.
The Angel of the World Invisible
Stood at my side, in glory like the sun:

"Thou kingly falcon," said the shape divine,
"Not in this world is nest or rest for thee,
This little planet packed with so great woes,
This star of tears, this country of sad eyes—
What is it, royal HAFIZ, thou hast done
That thou so drear a habitation chose!
Thy place is with the angel Gabriel,
High up within the boughs of Sidra's tree,
Upon the frontiers of Paradise.

"Hark! how thy name makes sweet the empty sky:
Over the brink of heaven the angels lean—
'HAFIZ, forsake the world,' I hear them sing;
'Bride of a thousand bridegrooms hath she been,
This ancient painted woman; the same lie
Hath she told all, nor yet in anything
Hath she kept faith; expect not constancy,
Enamoured nightingale, from such a rose.'"

So spake the angel to HAFIZ—even to me—
Here in the tavern at the evening's close.

34

When thus I sit with roses in my breast,
    Wine in my hand, and the Beloved kind;
I ask no more—the world can take the rest.
    Even the Sultan's self is, to my mind,
On such a planetary night as this,
    Compared with me a veritable slave.

No need of candles where my loved one is!
    Is not the moon of her bright cheek at full?
    Such eyes would fill with light the very grave.
No need of perfumes! the Beloved's hair
    Wafts such a fragrance to the feasting sense
That all this vinous tavern smells of myrrh
    And musk and ambergris and frankincense.

In this our order of the Magian creed
    Wine lawful is, but, were thy face away—
O rose that hath a cypress for thy stem!—
    We should on no account be drunk today.
Sweet is yon sound of ghittern and of reed,
    My head is all a-humming with soft strings,
And my heart full with the sad sound of them.

Talk not of other sweetness, love, to me,
    The vulgar sweets and sugars of the world,
My only hope of sweetness is in thee,
    And on that lip indifferently curled—
Saucy alike to beggars and to kings.

Beloved, blame him not if, for relief,
    The sanctuary of his ruined heart,
Nursing the precious treasure of his grief,
    Unto the kindly tavern HAFIZ brings;
Nor talk of shame to HAFIZ—for his part,
    Nowise ashamed is HAFIZ of his shame;
That which the world accounts a spotless name
    HAFIZ, indeed, would be ashamed to bear.
    Wine-bibber call him, and adulterer!
Go on! what else! he will not say thee nay.
    Is Shiraz then so innocent a place
That none but HAFIZ ever goes astray
    After the wine-cup and a pretty face?
Summon the Censor, he who takes such care
    Of us poor fools—he's always running after
Women and wine—the very same as we;
    Be sure he also loves good wine and laughter.

Nay, Sufi, go thy ways, let HAFIZ be!
    Tonight the never-ending fast is done,
And the great feast comes in with minstrelsy:
    Here shall we sit, until the rising sun
Glitters on rose and jasmine—I and she.

39

Preacher, it is all in vain you preach to me,
    Nor business of anyone's but mine
Where I have sinned and what my end will be.
    I ponder too on subtleties divine—
Pray solve me this: how Allah out of nought
    The waist of my Beloved made so fine
That it exists but in the lover's thought,
    Nor can be apprehended of the eye,
A metaphysic fancy of the mind—
    Solve me this riddle, preacher, how and why.

Again, you promise, when we leave behind
    This jasmined earth, its roses and its dew,
Eight paradises up there in the sky;
    I' faith, it makes a man in haste to die
To think of living after death with you!
    Listen! one corner of the earth with her
Is more to me than all the stars on high;
    Down here's my heaven, though yours may be up
        there!

What if to ruin all my life has gone?
    Upon that very ruin do I rear
    This building of my dreams, and very fair
Is it to dwell in and to look upon—
    This tavern-temple of the Thought of Her.
And, if to you my fate should seem unkind,
    Unjust my love, and oft-times harsh to me,
It is enough that she it was designed
    This exquisite anguish of my destiny.

HAFIZ is but a pipe for her to play;
    So that he feels the sweetness of her breath
Through all his being take its thrilling way,
    He heedeth not what any preacher saith;
And only when she takes her lips away
    Shall HAFIZ taste the bitterness of death.

42

My hermitage the tavern is—
Ah! such a pietist am I!
My abbot is the taverner—
Yea! such a pietist am I!
And every morning thus I pray:
Give us the red wine day by day,
God grant me too the sight of her!
Thus pray I to the taverner
Each morning at the break of day—
Such, *such* a pietist am I!

My matins are the songs I make—
So penitent at morn am I!—
Of sorrow for the night before.
So early is my heart awake,
That, long before the harp is heard,
Long ere the open tavern door,
I waken the still sleeping bird—
So early is my heart awake!—
With sound of my repentant tears.
So sweet the sound in mine own ears
Of mine own sorrow, that ere long
My heart is healed with mine own song;
And ere the middle of the day—
So early was my heart awake!—
My sorrow is all sung away.

Beggar and king to me are one:
So very beautiful is she,
That any beggar who shall fling
Upon her doorstep in a dream
Shall surely seem to me a king.

Whatever else I do or seem,
Only one thought possesses me,
In mosque or tavern—it is she;
Living or dead, or damned—it is she:
So very beautiful is she.

Better the beggar at thy feet
Than any king on any throne;
To be thy slave is very sweet;
The torture of thy tyranny
Riches and honour are to me;
Abased upon thy threshold-stone
I seem uplifted past the sun,
And none save death shall strike my tent
Of vigilant love before thy door.
Too well I know the fault is none
Of thine—it is mine for loving thee;
HAFIZ shall hold thee innocent
Before High God, and yet must he
Love thee for ever and more and more.

44

Last night, as half asleep I dreaming lay,
    Half naked came she in her little shift,
        With tilted glass, and verses on her lips;
Narcissus-eyes all shining for the fray,
    Filled full of frolic to her wine-red lips,
        Warm as a dewy rose, sudden she slips
    Into my bed—just in her little shift.

Said she, half naked, half asleep, half heard,
With a soft sigh betwixt each lazy word,
"O my old lover, do you sleep or wake!"
And instant I sat upright for her sake,
And drank whatever wine she poured for me—
Wine of the tavern, or vintage it might be
Of Heaven's own vine: he surely were a churl
Who refused wine poured out by such a girl,
A double traitor he to wine and love.
Go to, thou puritan! the gods above
Ordained this wine for us, but not for thee;
Drunkards we are by a divine decree,
Yea, by the special privilege of heaven
Foredoomed to drink and foreordained forgiven.

Ah! HAFIZ, you are not the only man
    Who promised penitence and broke down after;
For who can keep so hard a promise, man,
    With wine and woman brimming o'er with laughter!
O knotted locks, filled like a flower with scent,
How have you ravished this poor penitent!

48

No! Saki—take the wine away!
I have no need of it today;
    So drunk am I with adoration,
No longer have I any need
    Of commonplace intoxication.

How should a man whose eyes may drink
Her beauty, like the Northern Star,
    In a delicious meditation,
Remain contented any more
With common wine out of a jar!
No, Saki—take the wine away;
Though it were poured from heaven's brink,
I'd spill it on the tavern floor—
I have no need of it today.

Of course, I'll go on getting drunk,
But it will be another way—
    A more august inebriation;
And I'm afraid, old Magian monk,
You'll almost have to close your door
When HAFIZ buys your wine no more—
    That is the worst of reformation.

49

Now that the rose-tree in its dainty hand
Lifts high its brimming cup of blood-red wine,
And green buds thicken o'er the empty land,
Heart, leave these speculations deep of thine,
And seek the grassy wilderness with me.
Who cares for problems, human or divine!
The dew of morning glitters like a sea,
And hearken how yon happy nightingale
Tells with his hundred thousand new-found tongues
Over again the old attractive tale.

Yea, close thy books; let schools and schoolmen be;
Only a little lazy book of songs
Snatch up, and take the long green road with me.

Men left behind us, like that fabled bird
Anca, that dwells in Caucasus alone,
Remote from footfall, secure from human word,
We ask no company except our own:
For we are deep in love with solitude,
And green-leaved peace, and wildwood pondering—
Yea, even Love itself would here intrude;
HAFIZ would be alone with the sweet Spring,
HAFIZ would be alone with his sweet song.
Of the immortal lonely ones is he
Whom solitude and silence have made strong.
Therefore, he laughs at rivals such as ye
Who think to match his inaccessible fame;
Yea, you remind him, poor presumptuous fools,
Of that rush-weaver of the olden time
Who to the shop of a great goldsmith came:
Said he: "I too an artist am—for tools
Also I use, and keep a shop the same."
Yea, you too keep your little shop of rhyme!

53

Whose is yon candle of beauty?
    Whose the house that she makes so bright?
Ah! whose that enchanted window?
    Whose yonder fairy light?
My soul's on fire with its shining—whose
Is she? Ah! tell me whose!

Whose are the arms she lies in?
    Who watches her holy sleep?
Who are her friends and homefolk?
    Who dares for himself to keep
So fabulous a treasure? who?
Who is he? tell me who?

Whose the red wine of her red lips?
    Whose the cup she fills to the brim?
Whose all this fairy fortune—whose?
    Ah! God was good to him!
Delight of man's soul and body—whose
Is she? Ah! tell me whose!

Venus-faced, moon-pale, tell me
    Whose queen and whose pearl is she?
Whose jewel so precious, so priceless?
    Whose this wine that has maddened me—
Me, drunk without drinking? Tell me whose
Is she? Ah! tell me whose!

Who is the moth for yon candle?
    Who is he that was born to die
In that burning beam—ah! tell me who!
    Would God that it were I!
Vain is it, HAFIZ, to question who—
HAFIZ, it is not you.

54

I well could speak to her had I a mind—
Learnedly speak with Arab eloquence;
But eloquence to her would be unkind—
Wit before beauty is impertinence.
Her brows are like an angel's, but her eyes
Are like some devil's fallen from Paradise;
It is a strange paradox of Heaven and Hell:
Pondering on such a face the angels fell.

Surely you must not ask of me the cause
Why mortal beauty breaks immortal laws;
No reason can I give, save this alone—
That beauty's self for beauty's sins atone:
Reason enough, though reasonless it seems—
The lonely rainbow reason of our dreams.

Never the greatest man that yet was born
Has plucked a rose so soft it had no thorn.
Mohammed's self—great though his sacred name—
Found foes in friends, and his celestial flame
Was by the smoke of relatives made dim.
His friends took a long pilgrimage to him,
But his most bitter foe from Mecca came.

No barley-water monastery for me!
Monk of the tavern, my refectory
Is the cool silent cellar, snug with jars,
And my green bedroom has a roof of stars;
And when too close to me my sorrow comes,
Aleppo's vines and China's dreaming gums
Change my unhappiness to luxury.

Sufi, if I indeed offended you,
To wine, and not to HAFIZ, is it due;
Always am I offending in this way,
And every night and morning have I sworn
Repentance for last night and for—today!
And wished that HAFIZ never had been born.

O Saki, fill the wine-cup once again—
Today's repentance shall not be in vain.

59

Zahid, I beg you, leave my sins alone;
They are not yours—I'll settle for my own.

Each man a sinner is, and may be you,
O white-souled Zahid, are a sinner too.

If I be good—so much the better for me;
If I be bad—so much the worse for—ME.

Go be yourself, and your own business mind;
Within the universe is something kind

To sinners, Zahid, though you know it not.
Behind the veil, behind the veil. God wot,

Maybe the earthly saint is heaven's sinner,
And he who lost on earth in heaven is winner.

It matters not, O most misguided friend,
What little church or chapel we attend,

We all are seeking just the self-same thing,
And Love begins and ends our worshipping.

The world to come is good—indeed it is!
But so, believe me, holy one, is this.

Scorn not the joys you have for those you dream—
The shadow of a willow and a stream,

A face of ivory, a breast of myrrh,
And someone singing—Zahid, O beware

Lest you let slip realities like these
For theologic unrealities.

Talk not about your work—for what know you
The value of the little thing you do:

If you are kind, thank God that it is so;
If you are good—don't let your neighbours know.

But my poor poet HAFIZ, as for you,
What on the day of judgment will you do!
    Knock softly with a wine-cup on the door,
And be assured that they will let you through.

71

Without your cheek, black night is every day,
    Your cheek of roses made and shining dew;
      All life is dusty death that is not you;
There is no world with you such worlds away.

I wept so when last time we said goodbye,
    I washed from out my eyes the power of sight;
      That queen, your image, told me that she might
Dwell not in such a ruin as my eye.

So long as you were mine, my day of death
    Far in the distance, a mere fancy, loomed;
      Alas! now am I veritably doomed,
And measured out the wine-jar of my breath.

Stark near the moment is when I must die;
    Ah! love, from you far distant be the day
      When the dark watchers unto you shall say,
"Nothing is left of you in sea or sky."
Ah! then it will not avail that you repent,
    Or that you love me then; for I shall be
      A sighing dust, a grim anatomy,
A robe of ashes, an old monument.

My eyes with so much weeping are drained and dried
    Of natural tears; Beloved, if you would
      That still I weep, remaineth my heart's blood;
With tears of blood will you be satisfied?

Patience and laughter, HAFIZ; it is they
    Would be your doctors. Patience! how shall I,
      Dissolved in weakness, the power of patience try?
And sorrow and mirth met not this many a day.

74

Love is a sea that hath not any shore,
    And help upon that shoreless sea is none;
Who sails it sets his eyes on land no more;
    Yet gladly am I on that voyage gone—
    For ah! how good it is to sail that sea!
What though the longest trip at last be o'er,
    What though the proudest vessel must go down,
    My love is on the same big ship with me,
And when she drowns, I drown.

2

Talk not of reason to a man in love,
    Nor pit thy arguments against good wine;
Love has a wisdom wisdom cannot prove—
    Reason knows nothing of the things divine.

The happy heart can find its happy way,
    Nor its direction need of any ask;
I charge thee fill each moment of the day
    With love, as wine fills to the neck the flask.

Watch how the Saki brims our glasses up—
    So fill thy cup with living strong and deep:
    Leave not a dreg for death within the cup,
For no man goes on drinking in his sleep.

None but pure eyes may see the face I love,
    Scarcely discernible, as the young moon
    That like a spirit yonder walks above
The sleeping trees with little silver shoon.

Ask not who HAFIZ slew—ask but thine eyes!
  Nor yet the blame on heaven or fortune lay;
  Would I were certain that the dead shall rise,
Then would I come again for thee to slay.

I marvel at the hardness of thy heart;
  Strong stone is not so cold as its stern core,
  And the old rocks are softer than thou art:
But at the love that loves thee I marvel more.

75

Happy returns of this good day to thee,
  Saki! and, now that the long fast doth cease,
Do not forget what thou didst promise me,
  Whenas the wintry rigours of reform
  Should slacken and the world again grow warm,
  And the sour censor let us drink in peace.

Yea! Daughter of the Vine, forget not how
  With loyal hearts we battled might and main
To win thy freedom; ah! forget not now,
  In the rejuvenation of the feast,
  The friends that fought, and HAFIZ not the least,
  Faithful and firm, to make thee young again.

Still the old bloom is on thee—the same blithe ways!
  And in thy side the same warm heart doth beat;
Thank God! the wind of those inclement days
  In all thy garden killed no single rose;
  As to and fro the tavern my cypress goes,
How good again it is to hear her feet.

HAFIZ, the cup is like to Noah his ark,
  And Time the deluge is where all must drown;
  Quick! ere the torrent tears thy roof-tree down—
O hasten, HAFIZ, hasten to embark.

79

No one has seen thy face; a thousand eyes
    Are watching for the rising of thy veil;
    Rosebud, full many a foolish nightingale
Waits thine appearance with impatient sighs.

It is no wonder that I haunt thy door;
    Though far away indeed from thee I seem,
    That some day thou wilt love me is my dream—
Alas! it is the dream of many more.

Love is a church where all religions meet;
    Islam, or Christ, or Tavern, it is one;
    Thy face of every system is the sun—
O Sun that shines in the Beloved's street.

Where Love is there's no need of convent bell,—
    And holy living needs no holy frocks;
    Time ticks not to your monastery clocks;
Where goodness is there God must be as well.

Known to the Well-Beloved my sorrow must be,
    And all this anguish I suffer for her sake.
    For every other agony and ache
Doctor there is—she will my doctor be.

HAFIZ, God knows! not coward is thy cry;
    Reason enough there is for each sad word;
    If only thou wert certain that she heard!
So many a song is wasted on the sky.

83

O love, all hidden from my aching sight,
    May God have care of thee!
I miss thee all the day and all the night,
    Yet is my heart with thee.

Until my grave-clothes drag in the grave's dust,
My hand to touch thy healing hem I must
    Stretch out, beloved, to thee—
    The healing hem of thee.

O show me the prayer-arches of thy brows,
That I may raise my hand as in God's house
    And clasp the neck of thee.

Yea! if it needs must be that I must stand
Head-down in the burning Babylonian sand,
    Like the lost angel Harut, thou shalt see
    What sorceries I'll think of to bring thee.

Love, if for nothing else, grant me this grace—
    See how I ask it on this faithful knee!—
    That just a little moment we may meet:
So may I look once more upon thy face,
    And break my heart in tears upon thy feet,
        Big tears for me—and thee.

2

My bosom is a watershed of tears,
    All for the love of thee;
A hundred sobbing rivers take their rise

Within the brimming springs of my sad eyes,
    And all for love of thee.

Would that the desperate stream on thy heart's shore
    Might plant this seed I send of love—for thee,
And, waxing more and more,
    If there might shoot
    A million leaves from out that mighty root,
To show my love for thee:
O love, come plant the tree—
The love of me and thee.

3

Love, thou hast stabbed me with thy dagger eyes,
    There is no hope for me;
Bleeding in death, I for the doctor send—
    Doctor and murderer—*thee.*

O faithless doctor, do not seek to cure
    This hopeless case of me:
Go heal some other patient; all I ask
    Is just to die—for thee.

If in my eyes is any other face,
    O if my heart can hold one more desire
        Than face and love of thee,
Pluck out my eyes, and may the eternal fire
    Burn to white ash the faithless heart of me,
Faithless, O lovely one, to such a face,
    Faithless, O love, to thee.

Ah! HAFIZ, HAFIZ! wine and woman and song
   Is this thy love for me?
Well, well, dear profligate, do what thou wilt,
   I needs must pardon—thee.

100

Without a sign she went away;
    Weary she seemed of us—put on
Her garments hurriedly, took up
    Her burdens, and was gone.

Gone is she, yet no single kiss
    Upon her red lips did I lay,
Looked such a little on her face—
    And she has gone away.

I strive by many a magic charm
    To bring her back; yea, I rehearse
The Koran's wizard chapters, I
    Blow upon every verse.

"Never," said she, "will I forsake
    My friend and my companion";
True love I gave her—in exchange
    Secretly is she gone.

"Who loveth me himself must lose";
    So many a time to me she spake;
Thus not alone I lose myself,
    But her too—for her sake.

Proudly she walked the meadows green,
    A newly opened rose her face;
Alas! it was never mine to walk
    The meadows of her grace.

Yea, HAFIZ, it was not even thine
    Her parting face to look upon,
Nor might thou say farewell to her;
    And, HAFIZ, she is gone.

104

The Abbot of the Wine-house for thy friend,
Thou shalt have peace and pleasure without end;
So gracious he to all our vinous race,
In common gratitude we all abase
Our heads before him on the tavern floor—
It were superfluous to praise him more.
All the old fables men have ever told
Of Heaven's High Mansion builded all of gold
Pointed to this our Palace of the Vine,
Home of the ruddy daughter of the grape.
Misers for gold and silver sourly scrape,
But we of generous heart spend the red wine—
Misers and spendthrifts we of the red wine.

The wine-house garden is so fair a place,
So fresh the running stream, so soft the air,
I am content to sit a lifetime there.

O'er each man's brow God ran his pen of Fate;
We read the writing when it is too late.
With hidden treasure lurks the hidden snake.
Honour no man for birth, but his own sake;
Yea, honour him according to his deeds.
Whoso with understanding HAFIZ reads
Knows that he striveth ever, night and day,
After the good deed and the perfect way.

105

Who shall interpret the Beloved's hair!
So subtly caught, and coiled, and garlanded—
That maze, that glittering net, that shining snare;
Men of the true faith, and alike untrue,
Trapped in that cunning ambush on her head,
Are captive there—
It is but a little for such hair to do.

Thy beauty, love, is just a miracle,
An innocent gift that heaven gave to thee;
But ah! the uses thou hast put it to
Are downright sorcery.

Thy lips breathe out such healing that the time
Of Jesus is come back, and dead men rise;
So long thy locks, so strong, thy lovers climb,
Holding thereby, safe into Paradise.
On thy dark eyes a hundred blessings rain!
Though at each look indeed a lover dies,
Touching thy lips he comes to life again.

O wonderful astrology of love!
Thou science deep as ocean, and as high
As the last lonely light in yonder sky;
Hidden within the compass of thy lore
All folly of earth, all wisdom of heaven above,
Saving the knowledge how to love no more.

It was that draught out of the cup of love
That sent me to this other cup of wine;
HAFIZ, thy heart is captive—O beware
Lest thou thy soul lose too, and she entwine
Even thy faith in God in her long hair.

109

Beloved, it is not for you to question the words of the wise,
To say "Such and such is not so," or "It seems not good in my eyes";
Attend to your beauty, Beloved: it is there that your business lies.

To neither this world nor the next will I bow down this dream-filled head—
Ah, blessed be heaven that it put such dreams, such dreams, in my head!
But my heart—ah, what of my heart and its agony shall be said!

What is it inside my sad heart that cries out night and day?
It is not the voice of my soul—that hath never a word to say;
But something laments in my heart in a tossed tempestuous way.

I will suffer this pain no more, the veil of my patience is rent;
Ho! minstrel, thy melody bring, the heart's own medicament;
Yea, heal up my heart with the sound of some musical instrument.

Never that sad heart was set on the wealth of the world
 and its ways;
One thing have I asked of this life—to look day and night
 in your face;
My wealth was the thought of you, and my fame was the
 hope of your praise.

But now for a hundred nights my good sleep is all stolen
 from me;
In dreams I can find you no more, nor yet even the wine-
 house see;
Bismillah! of wine and wine-house should I ever forsaken
 be!

The tavern does me much honour because of my heart on
 fire;
What was it the minstrel played me last night on his sob-
 bing lyre?
The world passed away as he played; it was the voice of
 my heart's desire.

Its echoes still haunt with their sweetness the deeps of my
 dreaming brain;
Like the ache of wine in the heart is that aching half-lost
 refrain;
O mountainous heart of HAFIZ, that a song should rend
 thee in twain!

110

Helpless, we look for help—Sweet Heaven, save!
For pain like ours is there no remedy?
Is there no end to it this side the grave?

Our hearts we gave them, and our souls we gave;
There are no bounds to their rapacity;
Our very lives they seek—Sweet Heaven, save!

Helpless, we look for help—Sweet Heaven, save!
For mortal kisses an immortal price—
No less than our immortal souls—they crave.

Beautiful creatures of the lustful grave,
Ghouls of the sad necropolis of vice,
Drunken with dead men's blood—Sweet Heaven, save!

Helpless, we look for help—Sweet Heaven, save!
Dark is the night! will daylight never come,
And bring that union with my love I crave?

Endless the days and nights to grief I gave,
Yet each new day brings a new martyrdom;
Helpless is HAFIZ—can Sweet Heaven save?

121

Now that the rose is risen from the dead,
    And, at her feet upon the emerald lawn,
The violet hangs in worship her lowly head,
    To sound of singing drink the cup of dawn,
And kiss the Saki's cheeks a deeper red.

Ah! never in the time of roses be
    Without thy love and wine and the soft strings;
The rose's week is short—as short-lived we;
    Yea! hardly longer than a wild-bird sings,
Or rose is red, is our felicity.

See how the earth is spangled like a sky
    With starry belts of constellated flowers,
Responsive to the vernal stars on high;
    The tulip flames unquenched amid the showers,
And the enamelled earth with heaven doth vie.

In the rose-garden Nimrod lights his firespar
    Furnace of flowers for Father Abraham's feet;
Cast in the oven, the patriarch, said our sires,
    Turned the live coals into a garden sweet:
Good Magians, drink we as our law requires.

Old tales—with them O bother not thy head!
    And where the lost tribes went them let us leave—
Aad and Them'oud;—O little sweet-breathed maid,
    That tale of Jesus I can well believe—
How His sweet breath was wont to raise the dead.

And that old tale of Eden seems quite true,
    Since Spring has turned the world to Paradise,
With rose and lily thick and all this dew:
    Alas! so soon the fairy picture flies;
Days in the garden, why are you so few!

Who to yon bird can listen singing there,
    And doubt it is David in his heavenly throat?
Or see yon rose riding upon the air,
    And forget Solomon, who, our fathers wrote,
Upon the winds rode like a gossamer!

Asef grand vizier was to Solomon:
    Magians, come drink to great Imaddedin,
The Asef of the age; the paragon
    Of patrons unto HAFIZ hath he been—
A prince of largesse past comparison.

131

In the Beloved's path I laid my face,
    Yea! in the very dust of the highway
Bowed I my head—hoping a little grace;
    But she passed on her light indifferent way,
    Nor even deigned to notice where I lay.
God pardon her—she hath a lovely face.

God guard the careless creature from the sigh
    That broke unwilling from a bosom torn
    With grief of her intolerable scorn.
I had no other purpose but to die,
    Like an expended taper that at morn
Is blown out by a zephyr's passing by.

O very hard the heart of my beloved—
    Hard as a rock on which the bitter rain
Beats, yet remains unmelted and unmoved;
    O torrents of my tears! it was all in vain
Ah! all in vain the tears of the unloved,,
    And all unheeded all his lonely pain.

Last night so very bitterly I wept,
    All living things slept not for sympathy;
The very birds and fishes vigil kept;
    Awake was the wide world—save only she:
Ah! she alone it was that soundly slept—
    Though all the world was sitting up with me.

To the sad rain-song, HAFIZ, of your tears
Shut the Beloved's heart, and shut her ears;
But, HAFIZ, sing your happy songs instead,
And she would rise, to listen, from the dead;

Songs as wild honey sweet, that whoso hears
Sings each word over and over in his heart,
Lest he should lose of it the smallest part.

141

The days go by, yet not a word you send;
    Of aught befallen you no single word!
Tell the East Wind—he is our faithful friend;
    Or send a letter by some travelling bird.

Unless you come to meet me, how shall I
    The lofty region of your presence scale!
O angel, walk a little down the sky,
    And meet me, climbing, lest indeed I fail.

From jar to flagon hark how the wine goes!
    See that from flagon to cup it runs as fast!
And mark you how the coy and cloistered rose
    From her flushed cheek discretion's veil hath cast.

Not rose-leaves blent with honey over-night
    Would prove an unguent for my wounded heart;
Jay, but her bitter aloes, if I might
    Add but one kiss, would surely heal its smart.

Zahid, I often wonder that you dare
    To talk so much with such a drunken crew;
O Zahid, what if we should prove a snare,
    And have an evil influence over you!

Listen! at wine you've ranted long enough;
    For once in fairness then its virtues try;
Come, venture for yourself the perilous stuff—
    Taste it—and give us, if you can, the lie.

Poor devils of the wine-shop—be not fooled;
Trust only God and his good angel, wine;
Let not your own wine-wisdom be over-ruled
By each loud ignoramus of the vine.

Wisely our Magian Elder doth advise:
    The tavern's secrets unto none impart,
And never to the innocent advertise
    Experience of the tried and travelled heart.

HAFIZ to see your face burns night and day;
    O you, indulged by Heaven in every whim,
Turn not your head indifferent away,
    But in his desert throw one glance to him.

142

Life is not worth the trouble; the whole sky,
With all its pomp and pageantry of stars,
Was never worth the heaving of a sigh;
A tear indeed were paying far too high.
Yea! even all this goodly realm of Fars,
With Shiraz as the jewel in its crown,
Would find no merchant fool enough to buy
If Shiraz were not the Beloved's town.

Go sell your clouted prayer-coat if you can,
And see if any vintner counts it worth
A single cup of valuable wine,
Drawn from the musty cellars of old earth;
If so, you'll get more than I get for mine.
Yea! a prayer-carpet made in Turkistan,
Most excellent in colour and design,
For sale I offered in the vintner's street:
"All colours at once! O woven and dyed deceit!
For you exchange this cup of honest red!
Never!" the Abbot of the Wine-house said.

Dangers and hardships of life's troubled sea,
At first they seemed to me a little thing;
But ah! that weary old pearl-fishery
Hath more of perils nowadays than pearls;
Too strong its wicked current sucks and swirls:
It is not worth while—I let the others drown.

Yea! who would even choose to be a king,
And wear a royal crown upon his head,
If he must lose his head to wear his crown.
No, HAFIZ, it is a small world and a vile,
Not worth a second thought when all is said;
What if my heart low down has whispered—
"Even the Well-Beloved is not worth while."

143

Save the pursuit of faces like the moon,
Moonlit, moon-shaped, and moon-mysterious,
Which ever I follow, shod with flaming shoon,
I take no thought of anything at all.
Much counsel give I to my foolish heart
Touching a useful life expended thus;
But my heart takes no heed of it at all.
So take your counsel to some other mart,
Sufi, unless indeed you care to speak
About the down upon the Saki's cheek,
The fairy writing of a fairy tale;
For nothing else, indeed, that you can say
On other matters can the least avail.

I hug the wine-jar thus, and folk believe,
Seeing me bent in such a studious way,
I keep the Blessed Koran up my sleeve.
With all this smoulder of hypocrisy,
Some day I should not be surprised at all
If this old lying garment should take fire
And publicly proclaim me for a liar;
Surely it could not burn too fast for me—
The Tavern-Keeper takes no pay in prayers.

You who against the cup admonish us,
Thus making war on a divine decree,
Your very visage, dour and dolorous,
The pain of your own abstinence declares;
You do without-but how reluctantly!

Wine to the pure in heart is heart's delight,
Because its ruby no impression takes—

Saving the very face of sober truth.
As I talk on, as yonder candle bright,
I cannot keep from smiling 'mid my tears
To think of all this music my tongue makes,
This wasted eloquence she never hears.
Good Sufi, cease—you weary me in sooth!
You bid me take my eyes from off her face!
Deafen no more already deafened ears—
Take your tongue rather to some other place.

These mumbling incantations of your spleen
Are wasted—she's herself a sorceress,
As we all know who have her beauty seen.
Talk not of reason to a heart in pain:
I love her, but she loves not me again:
That's how the matter stands—no more, nor less.
Yea, and I glory in the skill that stole,
Most cunning fowler and swift hawk in one,
These wild birds of my body and my soul.

For God's love, to this dervish of your street
Alms of your pity grant, for doorstep none
Save yours approaches he, nor have his feet
On any other journeys ever gone.

So fresh and sweet these songs that HAFIZ sings,
They shall be young still when the world is old;
I often marvel that the King of Kings
Covers him not from head to foot with gold.

144

The face of my Beloved is a rose,
   Her hair a hanging garden thickly set
With curled and scented hyacinths in rows;
   Her cheek incarnadines the Judas-tree;
Fair as a sunrise in the golden net
   Of gossamered dawn, it glitters blindingly
Into my foolish Zoroaster eyes.
   Dainty as lily dust, the delicate down
In dimpled corners soft as shadows lies.
O Idol, Saint, Flower, Spirit, Miracle!
   Thy beauty is an everlasting crown;
God give thee everlasting life as well.

When first I fell in love with this dear girl,
   Methought that I had drawn up from the sea
Of all its rocking pearls, the heart's own pearl;
   I knew so little of the sea of Love,
This sea of blood that since has swallowed me;
Nor of the ambushed arrow of her eye,
   Which none escapes, knew I the mortal sting.
In a like case were all the great gone by:
   Yea, Kaikobad and Kaikhosru no less
On beauty's doorstep laid a foolish head;
   And all the mighty and immortal folk—
Poet, and conqueror, and sage, and king—
   Once wore, as we do, the Beloved's yoke.

Drink not with others and with me refuse!
    'Fore God, the Tavern-Master shall decide
If it is a proper way my love to use—
    That thou with all the others drink thy fill,
But only bring thy aching head to me.
O love, go not away; with me abide;
    Plant thou that stately cypress that is thee
Here by the running music of this rill
    That wells forever from my sorrowing eyes,
    A Ruknabad of unavailing sighs.

Trust not the rose, however sweet her smiles;
    The beauty of the world is in her face,
But all her hollow heart is filled with wiles.
    Ah! Nightingale, take warning by the case
Of those old dusty lovers, long since dead,
    Whose ashes from her labyrinthine hair
Upon the gossip wind at morn is shed;
    Lose not another singer in that snare.

She bade the East Wind tell not foe nor friend;
    But unto HAFIZ straight it brought the tale,
Which I by that same flutter-flower send—
    A nightingale unto the nightingale.

147

Beauty alone will not account for her;
No single attribute her charm explains;
Though each be named, beyond it glimmers she,
Strangely distinct,, mysteriously fair:
Hers this, this hers, and this—yet she remains.
Wonderful are her locks—she is not there;
Her body a spirit is—it is not she;
Her waist the compass of a silken thread;
Her mouth a ruby—but it is not she:
Say all other, yet hast thou nothing said.
Surely the beauty of houri or of fay
A fashion of beauty is—but to my eye
Her way of beauty is beauty's only way.

Unto this spring, sweet rose, pray draw anigh;
Sweet water it is—my tears—to water thee.

Thine eye, ah! what an arrow! thine eyebrow,
How strong a bow! and what an archer thou!
Ah! what a target hast thou made of me.

Love's secret verily no one man knows,
Though each in lore of loving deems him wise;
Love's like a meadow all aflower with Spring,
But in the shadow Autumn waiting lies,
And the wise bird is half afraid to sing—
A vanished song unto a vanished rose.

HAFIZ, a power strange to touch the heart
Of late hath stolen subtly in thy song,
Through thy firm reed unwonted pathos blows;
Her praise it is, and no new touch of art,
That gives this grace of tears unto thy song.

148

The Well-Beloved is very hard to please:
How to content her Heaven only knows!
Sometimes if playfully I touch her hair,
Thus with my hand, off in a tiff she goes;
Then, when I humbly seek to make my peace,
Her tongue's so sharp we almost come to blows;
At my wit's end am I to humour her,
So full is she of contrarieties.

Sometimes she lets a smile slip through her veil,
As the young moon sometimes an instant shows,
Scimitar-like, slashing a rift of cloud;
Then, like the moon, back in her cloud she goes.
Some nights so wakeful she, nought can prevail
On her to leave her wine and come to bed,
Though I for lack of sleep snore meekly, bowed
Over my empty cup with nodding head;
Yet in the day, let me begin a tale—
And instant fast asleep the baggage goes.

Love's is no easy way, be sure, to tread;
This soft and perfumed pathway of the rose
Is sown full thick with thorns for lovers' feet;
Well may he tremble who that journey goes.

Proudly the bubble rides upon the wine,
Buoyed up and boasting it of bubbles first;
Ah! learn this from its effervescent shine—
It is that same foolish puffing makes it burst.
So boast not of your beauty that groweth old;
Boasting is for the young and wonderful—
The strong gold sun on the young head of gold.

When the black scroll of your black hair turns white,
It will not grow black again because you pull
The white hairs out—it is Winter when it snows;
And, like the snows on yonder mountain's height,
These snows melt not for any kiss of Spring;
This Winter goes not when the Winter goes.

Your right to beg at the Beloved's door
Sell not to be a king upon a throne;
Its shadow is worth all the shining suns.
HAFIZ, if difficult the path you chose,
Its veil of mazy darkness is your own;
Happy the man for whom Love's highway runs
Clear in his sight, and unobstructed goes.

150

In the Beloved's Street I lost my heart!

HAFIZ had once a heart, Muslims, like you;
A pitiful good heart, a comrade true,
A counsellor, and a most faithful friend.

In the Beloved's Street I lost my heart!

Skilful it was to aid and to advise,
Shelter and succour, and exceeding wise
The broken hearts of other folk to mend.

In the Beloved's Street I lost my heart!

So, when I fell into Love's whirling pool,
Through the ensorcelled folly of my eye,
Upon my faithful heart did I rely
To snatch me back to shore. Alas! poor fool,
My heart had lost himself as well as I.

In the Beloved's Street I lost my heart!

The Street of my Beloved—it was there
I lost my friend: O perilous thoroughfare!
Most dangerous is my Beloved's Street,
And most detaining to the robe of man.

In the Beloved's Street I lost my heart!

O maze of honeycomb! O heavenly hive!
Wildered, I wander on with tangled feet,
Seeking my heart in the Beloved's Street;
But find again my friend I never can.

In the Beloved's Street I lost my heart!

Would I had pearls for every tear I shed!
Sometimes I wonder if he is alive,
And sometimes shudder lest he should be dead;
O never was a harder case than mine.

In the Beloved's Street I lost my heart!

Have pity, people! Honoured once and wise,
Before he drank of passion's fatal wine,
Was he who comes now in this beggar's guise;
So sweet the songs of HAFIZ used to be,
Ere my Beloved took my heart from me,
That multitudes would hold their breath to hear,
As at the singing of some heavenly bird.

In the Beloved's Street I lost my heart!

Perchance of HAFIZ you have sometimes heard
As of a man honoured in all the schools,
A man of sense, and of a judgment clear;
Believe it not-he is the king of fools.

In the Beloved's Street I lost my heart!

155

The rose is not the rose unless thou see;
Without good wine, Spring is not Spring for me.

Without thy tulip cheek, the gracious air
Of gardens and of meadows is not fair.

Thy rosy limbs, unless I may embrace,
Lose for my longing eyes full half their grace;

Nor does thy scarlet mouth with honey drip
Unless I taste its honey, lip to lip.

Vainly the cypress in the zephyr sways,
Unless the nightingale be there to praise.

Nothing the mind imagines can be fair,
Except the picture that it makes of her.

Surely good wine is good, and green the end
Of gardens old—but not without the Friend.

HAFIZ, the metal of thy soul is base:
Stamp not upon it the Beloved's face.

168

He who hath made thy cheek of the wild rose
    Can also give me patience, if he please;
And he through whom thy hair so thickly grows
    Can with as little trouble give me ease.

No hope had I of Ferhad from that hour
    When upon Shirin's lips his lips he pressed,
And threw the reins of passion to a flower,
    And took his joy—and left the world the rest.

What though the golden treasure be denied,
    He who gives gold and silver unto kings
Teaches the beggar to be satisfied
    To do without those bright superfluous things.

This world's a goodly bride to outward show;
    But, mark me! whoso taketh her to wife
As marriage portion must on her bestow
    No less a treasure than his very life.

Therefore, wise heart, 't were safer to abide
    In solitude, and to the cypress cling
That spreads its skirts upon the river side—
    And lo! the East Wind brings us news of Spring.

In the stern grip of Time my heart drips blood;
    Krwam-ed-din, I miss your august praise:
The golden hand which gave the parrot food
    Is closed against thee, HAFIZ, nowadays.

173

All the long night we talked of your long hair:
The hollow listening hours rolled darkly by,
The solemn world beneath the steady stars
To morning moved, sleep-walking up the sky;
Only in Shiraz in the realm of Fars
The dark night long kept open one bright eye—
It was where we sat up talking of your hair.

Each one of us, though wounded and far spent,
With arrowed eyelash sticking in his heart,
Still longed to see that bow your eyebrow bent,
And speeding yet another poisoned dart.
For it is so many days since we have heard
News of you, that our hearts grew faint with fear;
But now at last the East Wind brings us word:
Ah! blame him not—we had such need to hear.

Ere you were born love was not; through you fell
The bitter curse of beauty on the world—
Yes! it was all that hair upon your head;
Amid its crafty convolutions curled
All the dark arts of beauty lie in wait;
For even I, before I came to tread
That darkling way, among the saints did dwell,
And full of grace and safety was my state.

Open your tunic: I would lay my head
Upon your heart—ah! deep within your side
Silence and shelter sweet I ever found;
Else must I seek them in the grave instead.
When HAFIZ sleeps indeed beneath the ground,
Visit his grave—it was for you he died.

174

Time was your doorstep was my dwelling-place;
Mine eyes shone clear because of the bright dust
Raised by the daily passing of your feet;
My heart was pure with looking in your face;
Your soul's deep thought, that did my tongue repeat;
When Reason came with questions to the heart,
It was in your wisdom that I put my trust;
For had I fear that we should ever part;
And thus in the dear neighbourhood of you,
Society as rose and lily sweet,
Pure as a garden of lilies HAFIZ grew.

Alas! for my security gone by!
Beloved, wherefore have you stolen away!
Of doctor and friend I ask the reason why,
And question many another learned lip,
But no one hath a healing word to say.
Last night I went, seeking companionship,
Unto the tavern, and remarked how stood
The wine-jar with its foot set in the clay,
And its slim body filled heart-high with blood;
In a like case with yonder jar am I.

Abou Ishac, again, I thought upon,
So lately was he lord of Shiraz here;
But where today is Abou Ishac gone?
The ups and downs of this unstable sphere!
The city's laws his turquoise seals no more.

HAFIZ, 'twas only yesterday we heard
That strutting partridge noise his vanished state;
Blind, like us all, he saw not, foolish bird,
Poised in the clouds the falcon of his fate—
Alas! for his deserted palace-door!

176

Comfort thee, heart—this much at least is true
  Nothing forever lasts, and this thy pain,
Even as thy joy is gone, will leave thee too;
  Nothing remain
Of all this grief that is so near and new.

Though as the wayside dust to her art thou,
  Cherish not envy of thy rival's state:
It will some day be with him as with thee now;
  None to be great
More than a moment the high gods allow.

The brightest candle only shines till day
  Puts out the stars and candles of the night;
Be happy, little moth; burn whilst thou may:
  Her little light,
Ere thou art ashes, will have quenched its ray.

The Angel Gabriel and the lute's soft strings
  Alike have told me—nothing will abide:
In Jamshid's hall, at his high banquetings,
  Aloud they cried:
"Jamshid himself must die, though king of kings!"

What though thy lot be bitter as the sea,
  Make no complaint; or, be thy fortune fair,
Give thou no thanks—soon both alike will be;
And wherefore care
  What on life's page is writ—for who shall see?

In gold upon the mansion of the sky
   The stars write this last word for us below:
"The good deeds of kind hearts will never die;
   All else will go
With the spent candle and the butterfly."

HAFIZ, rejoice—look where at yonder door
   Stands the strange angel with his falchion drawn;
Death is he now—his name was Life before:
   They fear not dawn
Whom his hand smites, and their hearts ache no more.

192

The days of distance and the nights apart
    Are at an end;
All the long lonely Winter of the heart
    Is at an end:
No more forever shall the Autumn gloom,
No more forever shall December freeze;
For lo! the sweet swift-footed April breeze
Fills all the world with fragrance and with bloom—
    O my own love and friend,
    Our grief is at an end!

Our grief is ended and our joys begun;
We have climbed the night—at last we reach the sun;
And the wide world from pole to pole is bright
With the effulgent face of our delight,
    From shining end to end.

Deep in the scented shadow of your hair
    I bow my head and weep for very bliss,
So happy I can scarce believe me there—
    Too happy even to kiss;
For, love, O most desired and lovely friend,
    Through your great locks I see the rising sun;
The solitary night is at an end,
    Our morning is begun.

What care I if, for love of your fair face,
    To the wide winds my work and place I throw!
My work is just to love you, and the place
    Just where you are the only place I know.

Ah! to the wine-shop swiftly let us come,
With happy harp and loud exultant drum,
    And with a mighty voice the Saki call—
    "Deep cups and many, many cups for all!"
What matter how much money we shall spend,
For, O most lovely and beloved friend,
    Today the grief of HAFIZ, the long grief,
    In a wild blessedness beyond belief
        Is at an end.

194

O love, but I am sad at heart for thee."

"Have patience: very soon thy grief shall end."

"Thou art the moon—O be the moon to me!"

"I only shine two weeks, thou knowest, my friend!"

'Then on me shine."

                    "Who knows but it may be!"

"O fickle moon, I'll teach thee to be true."

"How could I be the moon, and constant shine?
Needs must the old moon change that she be new."

"Grow old, O moon, if only thou be mine;
I'll shut all other planets from my view."

"Thy fragrant locks have made me lose my way
About the world. In vain I seek a guide."

"Follow the way they went-who knows but they,
By the same fragrance, will bring thee to my side!
Have thou no fear, I shall be thine some day."

"Sweet is the breath that from thy garden blows."

"Sweeter the song thou singest, nightingale!"

"Tell me, kind-hearted, unrelenting rose,
When dost thou think my true love will prevail?"

"HAFIZ, ask not; till the time comes, who knows!"

207

O, I've good news for you—the Spring, the Spring!
    The blessed grass is green for one more year,
And all is piping and busy wing;
    Wild nightingales and roses everywhere.

Ah! when the money comes, I vow I'll burn
    This patched old saintly dervish coat of mine,
Like the young year be young too in my turn,
    And spend it all on roses and on wine.

For yesterday, in deep distress for drink,
    I took it to the taverner at morn,
Asking a cup of wine for it—and think!
    He said it wasn't worth a barley-corn.

See the red roses in the Saki's cheek,
    And on her garden-lips the violet blows;
No one has kissed me for a whole long week-
    O lovely one, grant me to pluck a rose.

My friend, before you wander in Love's street,
    Do not forget to take with you a guide—
So perilous for undirected feet
    The twists and turnings once you are inside.

Yet many wonders you will meet with there,
    And of the many this one not the least—
That there the timid deer it is pursues
    The lion, and pulls down the lordly beast.

And when in doubt of what to do or think,
    HAFIZ, raise high, drain deep, the golden cup:
Take counsel of the vine, HAFIZ, and drink
    At once the wine and the dilemma up.

Poor HAFIZ! After all, the Spring is gone,
    The roses and the nightingales are going;
Yet of the roses you have plucked not one,
    Nor drunk one cup of wine, for all its flowing.

223

What ails the times? Is friendship then no more?
　　What has become of the old kindly days?
　　　　The world seemed once so safe and warm with
　　　　　　friends—
New men, new ways.
And living went with gust; existence wore
　　Brave feathers, and the jocund planet whirled
　　　　Gaily in heaven: now somewhat sadly ends
That ancient world.

The water of life is muddied and bitter grown—
　　Clear as the immortal well it used to be;
　　　　The roses sicken and the breezes faint;
　　What aileth—me!
And when the roses bloom, they bloom alone:
　　No nightingales! I cannot understand—
　　　　What is the meaning of this mortal taint
Upon the land?

The world was once the birthplace of great kings,
　　And there was music in it and many loves;
　　　　But now hath Venus burned her lute y-wis,
　　And slain her doves:
No one gets drunk any more and no one sings;
　　No patron draws the ruby from the mine—
　　　　A melancholy world! HAFIZ, it is
　　No world of thine!

225

Once more red wine hath turned my willing head,
  O once again completely vanquished me!
Turned my old yellow cheek a rosy red—
  Blessings, red wine, on thee!

Blessings upon the hand, long since with God,
  That plucked the first grape from the primal vine,
And blest his feet that first the wine-press trod—
  True friend he was of mine.

When Fate has written 'lover' on thy brow,
  Accept thy doom; resistance is in vain;
Best to the tragic signature to bow—
  Fate rubs not out again.

Boast not of wisdom: hast thou ever thought
  That Aristotle must give back his mind
To death at last, even as the most untaught
  And savage of mankind?

Zahid, scold not, though fallen in arrear
  Our pious dues—we'll settle them some day;
It is no small sum—give us another year:
  God's debts are hard to pay.

This is the way to live—that when thou diest
  No one believes that thou art really dead;
HAFIZ, thy song the power of death defiest
  As long as rose is red.

HAFIZ is drunk in many different ways—
  Drunk with the Infinite, drunk with the Divine,
With music drunk, and many a lovely face;
  Also, he's drunk—with wine.

227

This house hath been a fairy's dwelling-place;
   As the immortals pure from head to feet
Was she who stayed with us a little space,
   Then, as was meet,
On her immortal journey went her ways.

So wise was she—yet nothing but a flower;
   Only a child—yet all the world to me;
Against the stars what love hath any power!
   Or was it she
Went softly in her own appointed hour?

The moon it was that called her, and she went;
   In Shiraz I had lived to live with her,
Not knowing she was on an errand bent—
   A traveller,
To sojourn for a night, then strike her tent.

How sweet it was on many a Summer's day
   On the green margin of the stream to lie
With her and the wild rose, and nothing say;
   Little knew I
That she was running like the stream away.

That was the sweet of life when, pure and wise,
   In her dear neighbourhood I drew my breath;
That was the truth of life—the rest is lies,
   Folly and death,
Since toward another land she turned her eyes.

Blame her not, heart, because she left thee so;
    The heaven of beauty called her to be queen;
Back to her hidden people must she go,
    Behind the screen;
Nor when she will return doth HAFIZ know.

232

A grievous folly shames my sixtieth year—
    My white head is in love with a green maid;
        I kept my heart a secret, but at last
    I am betrayed.
Like a mere child I walked into the snare;
    My foolish heart followed my foolish eyes;
        And yet, when I was young—in ages past—
I was so wise.

If only she who can such wonders do
    Could from my cheeks time's calumny erase,
        And change the colour of my snow-white locks—
    Give a young face
To my young heart, and make my old eyes new,
    Bidding my outside tell the inward truth!
        O it is a shallow wit wherewith time mocks
    An old man's youth!

Ah! it was always so with us who sing!
    Children of fancy, we are in the power
        Of any dream, and at the bidding we
    Of a mere flower;
Yet HAFIZ, though full many a foolish thing
    Ensnared thy heart with wonder, never thou
        Wert wont imagination's slave to be
    As thou art now.

236

The winds of March blow up the clouds of Spring,
    Heavy with flowers—O thou new-born year!
I, like thyself, am fain to dance and sing;
    But where, O where
Shall I the money find for wine and string?

Out on my empty purse! Didst ever see
    In any other Spring such girls as those!
They have bright eyes for everyone but me:
    Red little rose—
O for the money to buy one kiss from thee!

It is an illiberal age—O thou blue sky,
    For how much longer must I bear this shame!
Who ever had so lean a purse as I,
    With such a name?
Could I but sell my honour—I could buy.

Yet maybe better fortune is on the way:
    Last night I saw the true dawn on my knees,
As I for a great purse of gold did pray;
    The Pleiades
Mean money in thy purse—the old wives say.

The rose's hundred thousand laughters ring
    The garden through-a sweeter than herself
Hath she espied: no other bird doth sing
    Like the sweet pelf—
A rich man's in the garden, or a king.

Yet, Rose, what man hath made such subtle verse
    To honour thee? Ah, who hath flushed with fame
That haughty cheek, and taught men to rehearse
    Thy unknown name?
Enough of singing, HAFIZ! Fill thy purse.

HAFIZ, I know not who the arrow sped,
    Yet blood drips from the pinions of thy song;
For each small word thy heart hath surely bled,
    Silent and long,
And many tears it cost ere it was said.

249

I will not stay my hand till thou art mine;
    Not till my soul from out my body fly
Will I the hope of winning thee resign;
    And how can I
A new love take that am so wholly thine?

My life is at my lips, ready to go—
    O kiss those lips, and give me life again;
Hopeless my longing is, too well I know—
    But O the pain!
Beloved, would'st thou treat a beggar so?

When I am dead, go open thou my tomb,
    And a strange sight shall meet thy frightened eyes—
Flames feeding on me till the day of doom;
    And smoke shall rise
From fires of love that even my shroud consume.

If thou but walk the meadows, such delight
    Fills the sad cypress, that unnatural flowers
Break from its barren womb, and to strange height
    The low shrub towers—
Of thee so thaumaturgic is the sight.

Watch in yon garden how, from place to place,
    Seeking, the disappointed zephyr goes;
A rose he dreams of, lovely as thy face.
    Ah! no such rose,
Zephyr, in any mortal garden blows.

Beloved, raise thy veil; whole peoples mourn
    To see thy face, and men and women weep
And curse the tyrant day that thou wert born:
    How canst thou keep
A world in tears, and pay such love with scorn?

Set thick with barbed hooks thy tendrilled hair—
    No wonder fish are caught in such a net;
I bade my heart free of those hooks to tear—
    Ah! no-one yet,
HAFIZ, it answered, hath escaped that snare.

251–252

A caravan from China comes;
    For miles it sweetens all the air
With fragrant silks and stealing gums,
    Attar and myrrh—
A caravan from China comes.

O merchant, tell me what you bring,
    With music sweet of camel-bells;
How long have you been travelling
    With these sweet smells?
O merchant, tell me what yon bring.

A lovely lady is my freight;
    A lock escaped of her long hair:
That is this perfume delicate
    That fills the air—
A lovely lady is my freight.

Her face is from another land;
    I think she is no mortal maid—
Her beauty, like some ghostly hand,
    Makes me afraid;
Her face is from another land.

The little moon my cargo is;
    About her neck the Pleiades
Clasp hands and sing; HAFIZ, it is this
    Perfumes the breeze—
The little moon my cargo is.

253

Forget not, O my heart, thine ancient friends:
    The sweet old faithful faces of the dead,
Old meetings and old partings—all that ends;
    So loved, so vivid, and so vanished:
Forget not, O my heart, thine ancient friends.

The times are faithless, but remember thou
    Those that have loved thee, though they love no more;
Thou unto them art dim and distant now;
    Still love them for the love they gave before—
The times are faithless, but remember thou.

And the red wine remember, and the rose,
    And the old cry at dawn, the stream that ran—
In Paradise no sweeter river flows—
    Through banks of gardens on to Ispahan:
Yes! the red wine remember, and the rose.

The dead who kept our secrets remember well;
    They forgot much—we should not them forget;
Ah! HAFIZ, now they're gone, no man can tell
    Thy secret: it remains a secret yet.

254

What a musician is that rascal Love!
How out of wood and some six silly strings
Contrives he the very stones and trees to move;
And when he sings,
You hear the lonely stars listening above.

'T were a sad world without a lover's voice;
Their lamentations are as sweet as birds;
And, when the little creatures do rejoice,
What pretty words
The dictionary yields up to their choice!

O love, continue to sustain the pride
    Of this poor fly that dares to worship thee;
Mere hopeless love hath him so magnified,
    That seemeth he
A Bird of Paradise all rainbow-dyed.

No one could blame a king who, when he goes
    Abroad, finding forever falling from his sun
The shadow of some beggar, angry grows:
    So do I run
Beside the rose, the shadow of the rose.

Unto the leech I took my bloody tears:
    "What ails me, doctor?" unto him said I.
"It is love," said he, "and it may last for years—
    Yea, some men die;
But, borne with patience, it sometimes disappears."

HAFIZ, take heart; Love is a grievous lord;
    But this will always be the lover's creed,
Under the very shadow of Love's sword:
    No gentle deed,
And no sweet action fails of its reward.

255

In all this city not a girl for me!
    O girls and girls, but not the girl I mean.
If fortune be my friend, I trow that she
    Will take me hence— it is strange that I have seen
In all this city not a girl for me.

O for a light-heart sympathetic jade,
    In whom one's tender troubles to confide,
Say what one means no need to be afraid!
    O for the shelter of a woman's side!
O for a light-heart sympathetic jade!

2

My little gardener. Autumn comes along;
    Oft have I told thee, still hast thou forgot,
Doing thy beauty's rose such careless wrong:
    Death's wind is blowing, yet thou heedest not—
My little gardener, Autumn comes along.

Time's highwayman sleeps with wide-open eye;
    From his secure attack secure is none;
Today escape, tomorrow thou shalt cry
    Out upon all thy youth and beauty gone—
Time's highwayman sleeps with wide-open eye.

3

My song's a stage, I actors am and play;
    I make it all and watch it all alone;
Into my theatre, possibly, some day,
    A man with eyes may come, and make it known—
My song's a stage, I actors am and play.

4

To think I have been wise for forty years,
    And wrought so long and hard to make me wise;
Yet made a fool of by one glance of hers—
    Yea! lost it all for two narcissus eyes:
To think I have been wise for forty years!

No sorcery may match a miracle:
    Rivals of HAFIZ, a forgotten tale
Of Samiri, the conjurer, doth tell—
    How his poor arts against Musa once did fail:
No sorcery may match a miracle.

268

In the Heart's Market-Place go stand, my song,
And cry you "Oyez! oyez!" to all that pass,
Making this proclamation to the throng:
"All you that dwell in the Beloved's Street,
All you lost souls whose lives to her belong,
All you that beat your bosoms and cry 'alas!'
All you that follow her little wandering feet,
All you that kiss the dust where they have trod—
Hearken you all! Yea, for the love of God!

"There now is lost to us this many a day
The Daughter of the Vine, and none can tell
The way she took; all of her own desire
Hath she forsaken us, and gone astray
On some abandoned foray of sudden fire—
We needs must find her, or in heaven or hell!

"Her robe is red as rubies, as wine is red;
She wears a crown of bubbles on her head;
And she steals all the wisdom from the brain,
And all the manhood from the hearts of men;
Sleep not, lest she should take you unawares!
Whoso shall bring to HAFIZ back again
That bitter-sweet, wine-ruddied cheek others,
Will be rewarded with his very soul.

"A shrew is she, and hath a wicked tongue,
A wanton and a lover of the bowl,
A roysterer, a wanderer by night,
A loose-lipped wench of loud and ribald song,
Foul in her speech, lascivious of limb;
Yet very dear is she in HAFIZ' sight,
And, if you find her, bring her straight to him."

290

Wind of the East, pass by my Loved One's door,
   And bring me news of her—ah! bring me news
This do for Love's and one poor lover's sake;
   Do not refuse.
And, Rose, of thee this kindness I implore:
   As thy thanksgiving that thou art so fair,
Upon the nightingale some pity take,
   And grant his prayer.

Already was I loving thee when thou
   Wert but a tender slip of the new moon,
A little naked maiden of the sky,
   With silver shoon—
Not the deep-bosomed beauty thou art now:
   Ah! how I loved and how companioned thee!
Thou art a woman grown, yet still would I
   Thy playmate be.

If thou but love me, I thy name will bear
   O'er lonely seas to undiscovered lands;
Beauty, be wise, with gold and silver fill
   The poet's hands—
All future time shall dream of what you were:
   Such magical endurance hath his breath,
HAFIZ shall keep thy face a flower still
   In spite of death.

291

Show us thy face, and at the same time say:
"Moths of my candle, be prepared to die";
Parched are our lips with thirst—do not deny
The Water of Life: our heads down on the clay,
In the humility of death laid low,
Decapitated by a glance from thee,
Await the touch of our exulting foe,
When thou shalt brandish them in victory—
Or wilt indeed a little pity show?
And say: "His life was happy—he died for me."

White silver thy dervish hath not, nor red gold;
Yet scorn him not—his tears pure silver flow,
His wine-red cheeks are redder than any gold;
Ah! they are yellow too—with growing old.

Should the harp fail thee, and all woods that sing,
And aloes wood, indeed, be hard to find,
My heart for incense, my love for fire, I'll bring:
My body for thy censer was designed.

O come and dance with us, and the rest leave;
Draw from thy head the unbecoming cowl;
If not, O back into thy corner go,
And with the other dervishes go howl.

Draw off thy woollen coat, that Sufi lie,
And draw the red wine in; and straightway spend
Such gold and silver as thou hast lain by
Upon some little silver-bosomed friend.

My Friend! ah yes: fill all the sky with foes,
Against me be heaven and earth and hell allied,
Darken the earth with armies, thick as the rose—
I care not if my Friend is on my side.

Beloved, go not yet, but longer stay;
Here by the singing stream sit down and sing;
Thou fire and water and colour takest away,
Heart's love, and tears, longing and everything.

HAFIZ, the feast make ready; then invite
The Preacher, unto him our gladness show,
And say, as his starved eyes feed on the sight:
Canst thou again into the pulpit go?"

315

In the rose-garden of the World, one rose
    For me's enough;
Many a fairer in that garden grows—
    Mine's fair enough;
Out in the meadow all the shade I ask
    Falls from the cypress that I call my own;
O canting Sufi, take us not to task—
    Leave us alone;
      Weighty thy matter, but we find the stuff,
Most learned doctor, in this portly flask
    Heavy enough.

After a well-spent life comes Paradise,
With palaces fair painted on the skies;
We topers know a better heaven than this:
The tavern, to our wayward thinking, is
    Heaven enough.

Upon the margin of the stream we sit
    And watch the world with a contented eye;
The stream glides onward and ever, and so it
    As surely passes by.
Brief joy, long pain, is all the world can give;
    Pore on the stream and learn this lesson rough:
If you the gain, we find the loss, to live
    More than enough.

To sit with the Beloved, who could more
    Ask of a world so very sad as this—
Yea, even could a happier world give more?
    Ah, drive me not, Beloved, from thy door
    With harsh rebuff;

For knowest thou not thy doorstep is my home?
    Nor send me to some distant realm of bliss—
No knowledge crave I of the world to come,
    For never I of this old world that is
    Can have enough.

Union with thee! I have no other thought;
    In heaven's market I've no wish to buy:
Here I can see and handle what I've bought—
    Not so the rainbow wares of yonder sky.

It ill becomes thee, HAFIZ, to take huff
    At fortune, and her fickleness proclaim;
    Consider only thy resounding fame,
    Thy nature fresh and simple as a spring,
    And is not, HAFIZ, thy strange power to sing
Fortune enough?

317

Love, thou art fair—as delicate as dew
    Upon a rose-leaf thy young freshness is;
Holy with beauty art thou through and through,
    And strong in beauty as some stately tower;
A cypress in the fields of paradise
    Art thou, Beloved; thy mouth is a closed kiss—
    Would I were honey-bee to such a flower!
Happy the man whose grave is in thine eyes!
    How dost thou sweeten the surrounding air,
O hallowed creature, with thy virgin spice!
    Beloved, thou art fair.

Love, thou art fair; yea, all of thee is sweet;
    Thy brow is made of morning, and the grace
Of heaven falls over thee from head to feet;
    My future hangs upon thy little mole;
    I worship at the down upon thy face,
And only live because I die for thee;
Thou art compact of essences so rare,
To touch thee is my immortality—
    Thy body is my soul.
My heart reels with the sweetness of thy hair,—
    That sweet thick-lilied garden on thy head,—
And a rose-riot of fancy is my brain,
    Sweet thoughts! when were you on such sweetness fed!

HAFIZ, thy path of love is very plain,
  With many a rock and torrent hard beset—
Deserts and dangers all about thy feet,
  Death at the end, O faithful heart—and yet,
Because thy pilgrimage is made for her,
Thy lot, as thy Beloved is fair and sweet,
  Seems sweet and fair.

322

Shiraz, city of the heart,
    God preserve thee!
Pearl of capitals thou art,
    Ah! to serve thee.

Ruknabad, of thee I dream,
    Fairy river;
Whoso drinks thy running stream
    Lives for ever.

Wind that blows from Ispahan,
    Whence thy sweetness?
Flowers ran with thee as thou ran
    With such fleetness.

Flowers from Jafarabad,
    Made of flowers;
Thou for half-way house hast had
    Musella's bowers.

Right through Shiraz the path goes
    Of perfection;
Anyone in Shiraz knows
    Its direction.

Spend not on Egyptian sweets
    Shiraz money;
Sweet enough in Shiraz streets
    Shiraz honey.

East Wind, hast thou aught to tell
    Of my gipsy?
Was she happy? Was she well?
    Was she tipsy?

Wake me not, I pray thee, friend,
    From my sleeping;
Soon my little dream must end;
    Waking's weeping.

HAFIZ, though his blood she spill,
    Right he thinks it;
Like mother's milk it is his will
    That she drinks it.

330

How my heart aches with happiness tonight—
    Here by your shadowy side under the moon!
How strange your face is in the ghostly light—
    Under the willows underneath the moon.
    O spirit! O child! O unconceived bliss!
For this good night, kind Fates, we give good thanks.
We shall not know again a night like this
    Under the willows on the river-banks.

Love, shall I bid the Saki bring the wine?
    She waits but yonder underneath the moon;
I have already drunken deep of mine,
    Here at these stars—just underneath the moon.
Ah! how it tips the tongue with witty fire,
    And makes one's fancy play a thousand pranks!
O! I could sing—yea! will I to this lyre,
    Under the willows on the river-banks.

The fairest Jewels of my purest thought
    Here will I deck you with under the moon—
Strange deep-sea pearls up many a fathom brought
    From my deep heart, far underneath the moon;
And from Earth's centre my spirit shall bring to light
    Gems without name and number for my bride—
The bride that nature gave me, this fair night,
    Under the willows on the river-side.

How sweetly runs the river round yon bend—
    O Ruknabad is fair under the moon!
Would that this night of nights might never end,
    Or we might die thus underneath the moon!
Too soon shall morning take the stars away,
    And all the world be up and open-eyed,
This magic night be turned to common day—
    Under the willows on the river-side.

HAFIZ must throw him rue upon the fire,
    Lest, for this happy night under the moon,
The evil eye of envious desire
    Fall on him, singing underneath the moon.

331

For all her cruel grown-up ways,
    My love as yet is but a child;
She counts but fourteen little years
    That hath this famous heart beguiled,
And all these salt and sounding tears—
    I shed them for a child.
A child that knows not wrong from right,
    A baby fallen from the moon;
Pity she knows not yet, nor love—
    Pray God she knows them soon!
Else will she slay me some fine day
    In childish innocence of sport,
And be acquitted for the sin
    By the most learned court—
For she as yet is but a child.

Her heart still sleeps; still sleeps her mind;
    Nor false from true, noble from base,
Can she distinguish or divide;
    All of her sleeps—except her face.
Yea! she I love is such a child,
    For all her beauty slim and silk,
That still there lingers on her lips
    The sweetness of her mother's milk.

Ah! idol—with your fourteen years,
    And all your young alluring grace,
HAFIZ were wise to hide his heart
    Away in some safe place.
Alas! already it is too late—
    My heart is lost this many a day:
After the newly opened rose

    That nightingale has flown away.
If she I love breaks hearts like this,
    Thus vanquishes strong men and hard,
The Sultan would be well advised
    To make her Captain of his guard;
For such a might is in her eyes
    To break the strong and curb the wild
One look—and you shall bleed to death!—
    And she as yet is but a child.

353

"I will get drunk," saidst thou, "and kiss thee twice":
That was the promise thou didst make to me,
The time is now gone past this many a day;
Thou and thy solemn promise still delay,
Nor have I sign of kisses nor of thee—
"I will get drunk," saidst thou, "and kiss thee twice."

"I will get drunk," saidst thou, "and kiss thee twice":
So ran thy promise—yet of two, not one,
Not half a kiss, nor e'en the smallest part
Of kiss most fugitive have I, sweetheart!
Ah! whither art thou and thy promise gone!
"I will get drunk," saidst thou, "and kiss thee twice."

"I will get drunk," saidst thou, "and kiss thee twice":
Ah! bring that tiny pert pistachio
Thou callest mouth and let its sweetness out;
So small it is, some people are in doubt
Whether indeed thou hast a mouth or no!
"I will get drunk," saidst thou, "and kiss thee twice."

"I will get drunk," saidst thou, "and kiss thee twice":
Try not my patience, woman, over long:
HAFIZ is not the man to be denied,
Nor will he suffer such as thou deride—
So small a woman—so great a lord of song!
"I will get drunk," saidst thou, "and kiss thee twice."

"I will get drunk," saidst thou, "and kiss thee twice":
HAFIZ is not a man for thee to flout;
Yea! should the sky itself such insult dare,
Down from their stations the strong stars I 'd tear,
And turn the very heavens inside out!
"I will get drunk," saidst thou, "and kiss thee twice."

361

O love that stole my heart with your strange face,
    How pitiless you are, how pitiless!
    Cruel to me, but cruel none the less
To the wide world, that, in the same sad case,
Loves you as I, and loves and loves you, love.

Sometimes I sigh as though my heart would break—
How red your lips are, O my love, my love!—
    And sometimes pluck the arrow from my heart;
    But, heartless one, what is the use to tell
The torments that I suffer for your sake
    To you that could be heaven, instead of—hell;
    O heartless one, to whom I gave my heart!

And, Love, alas! alas! alas! for me!
    Each day you grow more fair,
        Each day your face, even as the maiden moon
    Thrives like a flower upon the midnight air,
Brims with more beauty like a silver spring;
Ah! love, but how compare to anything
    Beauty beyond description or compare!
    A face which as its eager captive takes
    A soul like mine, and such a great heart breaks:
face of faces, think how fair must be
    The face that conquers HAFIZ—O my moon!

364

This moment on the air strange sweetness came,
   From the Beloved a faint far-travelled balm,
   And the wide Summer midnight sleeping calm
Opened in one deep hall of sudden flame;
Alight an instant each slow-moving mile,
   Distance leapt into daylight and was gone,
And for an instant, fleeting as her smile,
   I saw the camels slowly moving on.

Unload, O camel-drivers, your rich freight,
   Your costly spices and Arabian gums;
   The North Wind surely tells me that she comes—
Nor body nor soul can any longer wait.

Ah! Summer lightning, plainly you foretell
   That Summer of the soul when there shall leap
Lightning from heart to heart, and all be well
   Down in the silence of the soul's great deep.

Be not impatient, heart, nor more complain,
   For the Beloved that was so long away
To you and pleasant Shiraz comes again
   With wonder at the dawning of the day.

Come, for the seven rainbows of my eye
   Are red with tears of blood because of thee—
The rose's colour and the heart's own dye;
   Hung with my tears as with a tapestry
The workshop of fair sight—thy holy place.
   Come, for my famished heart's one aching thought
Is of that fabled mouth that in thy face
   Mathematicians would define as nought,

That seed-pearl of invisibility—
    Think of a man who spends his life in vain
Seeking a mouth too small for him to see:
    Will the wide world see such a fool again!

HAFIZ, the loved one's yoke is hard to bear,
    And none there is thy great love to console;
Is HAFIZ never angry then with her?
    Is a man angry with his very soul?

For love of thee, HAFIZ is surely dead;
    Yet fear thou not to come anigh his grave;
Lawful it was in thee his blood to shed;
    Read thou his epitaph: HAFIZ FORGAVE.

365

Whenever I of the Beloved sing,
So subtle and so sweet becomes my tongue,
Astonishment I see on every face
To hear the milk and honey of my song.
"From Heaven it came, and from no other place,"
Sometimes I hear them softly whispering,
"That speech as plenteous as camel's milk
When evening gathers in the swollen herds."
So from the pent-up udder of my heart
Rushes this milk-white cataract of words.

"Ah! when wilt thou have mercy upon me,
When show some kindness to this sorrowing heart!"
"It is life, not I, that am unkind to thee!'
Answered my love: "Life forces us apart.
Blame not the beauty of a woman's face
For the stupendous wrongs of Time and Space."
Ah! well did Mensour on his gibbet sing:
"The priest knows nothing of the things divine."
None but the lover knoweth anything
Of loving, or of sorrow such as mine.

To a dear friend I gave my heart away—
A saucy quean good to look upon;
But O! the tears I've wasted since that day
With Noah's flood would bear comparison;
Yet doth her image on my heart remain,
Washed not away by all that bitter rain:
Though nowadays I never see her face,
And am forbidden to approach her door,
Trying in vain all avenues of grace.

Only a little while ago I swore
The hand of HAFIZ was a potent charm
Against evil spirits and the evil eye,
And proffered it to shield her neck from harm;
But she disdained its properties to try.

HAFIZ, methinks, at last thou growest old:
Loving and drinking were so easy once,
A mighty wencher wert thou in thy day,
But now at both thou art a perfect dunce;
Now is thy soul aweary, thy warm blood cold,
And all thy spirit wasted quite away.

378

Love, I am like the candle
That burns all night for your sake;
In the morn of your smile I flicker and fade—
Yea! go right out for your sake.
So deep and so sweet is the yearning
Of that lonely candle burning,
That when I am dead
A violet bed
Of my longing heart shall be made.
O my true heart shall break
In blossom for your sake!

I lifted my eyes to your threshold,
In hope of a look or a word;
But you thrust me away from your threshold,
Unlocked on and unheard.

O faithful hosts of sorrow,
I bid you all good morrow,
For only you
To me are true;
Lonely, without a friend,
On you can I depend;
From you can always borrow,
My faithful sorrow.

Slave of the iris of my eye,
Black devil though he be,
Slave of his friendliness am I,
His ready sympathy;
For every beauty that I see
He sees it too,

And every tear that I may shed
For love of you—
He sheds it too.

My idol's beauty is displayed
In every place;
The whole wide world can look upon
Her lovely face;
My idol greedily accepts
All kinds of praise;
Yet, though by all she be desired
With foolish eye,
Only by me
With proper praise is she admired;
I only see
What thousands look upon
And never see—
I, only I.

HAFIZ, when deep down in the grave you lie,
Merely the zephyr of her passing by
Your little stiff and solitary room
Will set your mouldering heart beating so loud,
That you will tear a way out of your shroud,
And leap alive and laughing from the tomb!

384

Heavens! do you think this is a time to choose
    To give the good wine up?
Just at the very moment when the rose
    In every garden blows!
How can I so unseasonably refuse
    The Spring's own cup?

Nay—call the minstrel! So with lyre and reed,
    Roses and girls, and girls, and song and song,
I may at length my hoarded virtue use,
    Ah! hoarded up too long!
For I am sick to death of all the schools,
And now at last, at last, that I am freed
    Awhile from wisdom's fools,
    Ah! full advantage of it will I take,
And my deep thirst for beauty and for wine
    For once, at least, I'll slake.

Talk to me not about the Book of Sin,
    For, friend, to tell the truth,
That is the book I would be written in—
    It is so full of youth.

And, mark me, friend! When on the Judgment Day
    The black book and the white
    Are angel-opened there, in Allah's sight,
        For all to read what's writ;
Just watch how lonely the white book will be!

But the black book, wherein is writ my name,—
  My name, my shame, my fame,—
With busy readers all besieged you'll see,
Yea, almost thumbed away—
    So interesting it.

And as for this, my fatal love of wine,
Believe me, friend, it is no fault of mine—
It is fate, just fate; and surely you don't think
I fear a God that destined me to drink?
This life of HAFIZ was the gift of God—
  To God some day I'll give it back again;
Ah! have no fear! when HAFIZ meets his God,
  I know HE will not call it lived in vain.

440

At sunset, when the eyes of exiles fill,
    And distance makes a desert of the heart,
And all the lonely world grows lonelier still,
    I with the other exiles go apart,
And offer up the stranger's evening prayer.
    My body shakes with weeping as I pray,
Thinking on all I love that are not there,
    So desolately absent far away—
My Love and Friend, and my own land and home
    O aching emptiness of evening skies!
O foolish heart, what tempted thee to roam
    So far away from the Beloved's eyes!
To the Beloved's country I belong—
    I am a stranger in this foreign place;
Strange are its streets, and strange to me its tongue
    Strange to the stranger each familiar face.
It is not my city! Take me by the hand,
    Divine protector of the lonely ones,
And lead me back to the Beloved's land—
    Back to my friends and my companions.
God of the strangers, set once more my feet
    Upon the merry home-returning way;
Ah! the good hour when in the wine-house street
    My gonfalon I once again display!
Not a soul knows me in this desert place—
    Saving the winds of heaven I have no friend;
O to be back where someone knows my face,
    And in the old haunts all my money spend!

When I come back, my youth will come back too,
    And, little mistress, when we wander wild
Among the meads, so mad I'll be, that you
    Will seem the grown-up one and I the child.
O wind that blows from Shiraz, bring to me
    A little dust from my Beloved's street;
Send HAFIZ something, love, that comes from thee,
    Touched by thy hand, or trodden by thy feet.

453

Wouldst know what fortune is? Fortune for me
  Is to behold the face of her I love,
    In the same street of the same world to dwell;
  Ah! far above
The hollow state of kings and princes he
  Who at her doorstep begs his daily bread—
    What should he buy who hath all heaven to sell,
  Or eat, being fed?

To leave the world were easy—just to die,
  And draw no more thy unconsidered breath;
    Ah! but to leave thy love behind, it is this
  That makes death—death.
And so. Beloved, therefore it is that I
  Make haste to kiss thy rose, for who can say
    It will bloom tomorrow, or I come back to kiss
  Another day.

HAFIZ, guard well this treasure of thy friends;
  Love them well now, and well their voices learn;
    Soon shalt thou hear them only in thy dreams—
  None may return
Who from this two-doored house of living wends:
  Down in the grave is no companionship;
    None talks, none listens, no eye with kindness
    beams,
  No hand to grip.

457

The Princess of the box-trees, she that vies
In stature with that straight and shining tree,
And queen of those the lashes of whose eyes
Abase the strength of captains, yesterday
Met me, her humble dervish, in the way;
Drunk and transfigured with red wine was she.
She spake, and sweet her glance upon me fell:

"O eye and lamp of our sweet Persian tongue,
That empty purse I see thou carriest still,
Stranger to gold and silver as of yore!
Give me thine ear, O dervish-I will tell
How thou its lean and shabby paunch may fill,
To fill it hear a quicker way than song:
Be but my slave, and thou art poor no more.

"Be but my slave, it shall be thine to eat
Of all the silver fruits of this fair tree;
This garden shall be thine from head to feet;
Be but my slave, and thine its golden key.

"Thou art too fearful—not so humble thou
As yonder mote that dances in the sun,
Yet in the golden vortex of far fire
At last it whirls along, its journey done;
Be but my slave, and like it thou shalt be
Swept up into the heart of my desire."

She ceased, and I, continuing my way,
Unto a meadow set with tulips came.
"East Wind," I asked, "who are these martyrs, they
That in their bloody shrouds stand here aflame?"

"I know not," the wind answered; "none can say.
HAFIZ, a sacred mystery is this:
Pursue it not, lest, HAFIZ, thou shouldst miss
A wisdom thou dost surely understand.
Of little silver bosoms be thy song,
And Venus faces, and small silver chins;
Such are the themes best suited to thy tongue.
Take thou the wine-cup firmly in one hand,
And with the other unto Heaven cleave;
Satan behind thee, cleansed of all thy sins,
The mysteries to the Beloved leave."

465

Deep in my heart there dwells a holy bird;
   O but it is weary of its earthly cage,
     And in the dark of the body sadly sings;
  Its heritage
Is the ninth heaven; its right is to be heard
   Before high God; its royal nest should be—
     For wide as the empyrean are its wings—
  The Sidra tree.

When from the dunghill of this world it flies,
   Bird of the soul, it stays not in its night
     Till on the top of heaven it proudly stands,
  Far out of sight
Of the sad straining of our mortal eyes;
   And wheresoever its rainbow shadows rest,
     The folk go happy in those favoured lands
  From East to West.

This earth, the lonely footstool of the stars,
   Is not thy place, O HAFIZ; nay, such songs
     Should fill the listening palaces of heaven;
  To God belongs
Thy voice, sweet bird, behind these fleshly bars;
   Thy singing pastures are those fields on high,
     Heaven's roses and the dew that falls in heaven—
  Bird of the sky.

477

In the green sky I saw the new moon reaping,
    And minded was I of my own life's field:
    What harvest wilt thou to the sickle yield
When through thy fields the moon-shaped knife goes
    sweeping?

In other fields the sunlit blade is growing,
    But still thou sleepest on and takest no heed;
    The sun is up, yet idle is thy seed:
Thou sowest not, though all the world is sowing.

Back laughed I at myself: All this thou'rt telling
    Of seed-time! The whole harvest of the sky
    Love for a single barley-corn can buy,
The Pleiads at two barley-corns are selling.

Thieves of the starry night with plunder shining,
    I trust you not, for who was it but you
    Stole Kawou's crown, and robbed great Kaikhosru
Of his king's girdle—thieves, for all your shining!

Once on the starry chess-board stretched out yonder;
    The sun and moon played chess with her I love,
    And, when it came round to her turn to move,
She played her mole—and won—and can you wonder?

Earrings suit better thy small ears than reason,
    Yet in their pink shells wear these words today:
    "HAFIZ has warned me all must pass away—
Even my beauty is but for a season."

483

Dawn, like a lover, the black robe of night
    Rends, and the naked shining of the sky
Gleams here and there in gashes of torn light:
    How often I
Have rent my tattered robe from left to right!

Sweet blows the morning breeze—it blows from thee,
    Sleeping at dawn with little fluttering sighs;
Thou happy bird, O sing the way for me
    To where she lies—
For tears I can no more the pathway see.

So thin grow I with longing, and this ache
    That in the grave will now be ended soon,
The folk at evening my pale body take
    For the new moon—
Being like a thread of silver for thy sake.

When in this world my face no more is seen,
    Faded with too much loving of thy face,
Look not upon my grave for grasses green,
    But in their place
The blood-red rose will tell what I have been.

Shame on me that I still can breathe and live,
    Unloved by thee—O foolish heart, be still!
Beloved, wilt thou this affront forgive?
    Soon HAFIZ will
Those rebel pulses their quietus give.

487

With last night's wine still singing in my head,
I sought the tavern at the break of day,
Though half the world was still asleep in bed;
The harp and flute were up and in full swing,
And a most pleasant morning sound made they;
Already was the wine-cup on the wing.
"Reason," said I, "it is past the time to start,
If you would reach your daily destination,
The holy city of intoxication."
So did I pack him off, and he depart
With a stout flask for fellow-traveller.

Left to myself, the tavern-wench I spied,
And sought to win her love by speaking fair;
Alas! she turned upon me, scornful-eyed,
And mocked my foolish hopes of winning her.
Said she, her arching eyebrows like a bow:
"Thou mark for all the shafts of evil tongues!
Thou shalt not round my middle clasp me so,
Like my good girdle—not for all thy songs!—
So long as thou in all created things
Seest but thyself the centre and the end.
Go spread thy dainty nets for other wings—
Too high the Anca's nest for thee, my friend."

Then took I shelter from that stormy sea
In the good ark of wine; yet, woe is me!
Saki and comrade and minstrel all by turns,
She is of maidens the compendium
Who my poor heart in such a fashion spurns.
Self, HAFIZ, self! That must thou overcome!

Hearken the wisdom of the tavern-daughter!
Vain little baggage—well, upon my word!
Thou fairy figment made of clay and water,
As busy with thy beauty as a bird.

Well, HAFIZ, Life's a riddle—give it up:
There is no answer to it but this cup.

491

What ails thee, Saki! Wine, for God's love, bring
Whoever saw an empty cup in Spring!

Hast thou forgot this is the drinking season?
The rose is back again: what better reason
To fill the cup, and fill the cup again!
Mind you, we'll have no drinking out of season!
But not to drink in Spring is arrant treason—
So fill the cup, and fill the cup again!

What ails thee, Saki! Wine, for God's love, bring!
Whoever saw an empty cup in Spring!

'Fore heaven, with all this piety and fast,
But it is good to get a drink at last!
My very heart-strings shrivelled are and shrunken;
I wonder, Saki, that they didn't crack.
O! but I'll soon feel better when I've drunken:
Now life begins again—for Spring is back.

The very Sufi who but yesterday
Enlarged upon the error of my way,
Himself so drunken is with the good Spring—
I saw him to the winds his virtues fling,
And heard him all his piety unsay.

What ails thee, lover! Where is pipe and string?
Whoever saw so long a face in Spring!

Only a day or two the rose is ours,
Only a little while Musella's bowers;

Lover, make haste some smooth-cheeked girl to choose,
And in thy kissing not a moment lose:
Nothing but faces fade so fast as flowers.

Music, O minstrel! Wine, O Saki, pour!
The rose will soon be gone, though we remain;
Soon, ah! so soon, the merry Spring be o'er—
So fill the cup, and fill the cup again!
Mark thou the Saki's cheek reflected there—
Was ever anything on earth so fair!

What ails thee, lover! Where is pipe and string?
Whoever saw so long a face in Spring!

Minstrel, when you before the sultan sing,
Thy song must be of HAFIZ' fashioning:
No other songs are worthy of a king.

493

What hast thou done! Thrown thus thy virgin shame
 Upon the winds! With naked eyes on fire,
  Forth from the house, veil-less, I saw thee run,
 And hot desire
Burned in thy maiden cheeks, and drunken flame;
 The East Wind made a wanton of thy hair:
  little love, what is it thou hast done?
 And thou so fair!

To think that thou art anybody's girl
 That dares to cast lascivious eyes on thee!
  Thou such a queen! The very beggars now
 Can mock at me,
Who might not even touch the tender curl
 Upon thy head. Ah! that mysterious zone,
  And all that fragrant treasure that was thou,
 Quite common grown.

We all played for thee, with our hearts for dice;
 Tricked are we all. O stone that seemed a heart,
  Will thou be stone forever? Come what may,
 To me thou art
All beauty still, which whoso dreams he buys
 More foolish is than HAFIZ, when he thought
  To buy with love. Ah! let the dotards pay—
 Thou art not bought.

495

Strange heart, the way is open—yet thy feet
    Will take it not; it is but for thee to go
In any hour to the Beloved's Street,
    And say: "I know That thou art mine. I take thee, as is meet."

The game is thine, if only thou wouldst play
    This polo of the heart; luck, like a mall,
Is in thine hand; thou makest no assay
    To strike the ball;
Thou holdest back thy falcon from its prey.

This red blood in thy veins that idly flows,
    Why dost thou use it not to dye her cheeks
With crimson of her love's surrendered rose!
    Thou art too meek—
Such hesitation like a coward shows.

How canst thou watch such wine untasted sink
    Where thou hast spilled it, thankless, in the dust!
Ah! some day, sick for wine, but thou shalt think
    How once thou thrust
This willing cup away, and would not drink.

Strange heart of HAFIZ, say what this may mean—
    To the Beloved's court the world doth bring
Its homage, and the beauty of thy queen
    All others sing:
Absent and silent only hast thou been.

524

Two gallons of old wine, and two old friends
    That know the world and well each other know,
        A corner of the meadow, an old book,
    A river's flow:
In such simplicity begins and ends
    All that I ask of God—keep all the rest,
        Luxurious world, but leave me this green nook;
    I keep the best.

Unquiet are the times; in what rude hands,
    Shiraz, is fallen thy beloved rose!
        Yea! and these war-worn eyes of mine did see
    Thy savage foes
Ride with my own true love to other lands.
    So heaven repays its servants! Well, red wine
        There still remains to comfort thee and me,
    Old friend of mine.

Here let us sit until the storm be passed;
    In all the meadows scarce is left a flower,
        So fierce a whirlwind smote our little town,
    Wild to devour—
Patience! God will not suffer this to last:
    The times are sick, and none knows who shall cure;
        Best, HAFIZ, in the cup thy griefs to drown
    And so endure.

537

The mercy of God, so long as there is day
    To follow night, till the last morning break;
        The mercy of God, so long as the sweet strings
    One with another a sweet union make;
On Arak and the little house I pray
    That on the corner of the hill-side stands,
        Above the winding stream that scarcely sings
    For the deep sands.

I am the man who prays for whoso fares
    Lonely about the world; the folk that go,
        Lost for a friend's hand or a woman's breast,
    On aching journeys; and for all who know
No lights at evening, put I up my prayers.
    Ah! but there is one lovely traveller
        For whom I pray more than for all the rest—
O harm not her!

Longing for news of her, I am as dead:
    O messenger, thou art a weary while!
        My love! my love! in every place thou art
    My home, my peace; my life is in thy smile,
As the mote's life in the sun, and comforted
    Is all my changing state remembering thee;
        Still at the judgment this old naming heart
    Thy heart shall be.

How dare I set my hopes on such a queen,
    Being what I am! HAFIZ, hast lost thy wit?
       Rakehell and profligate, resounding word
    For evil living, yea! and proud of it;
Incarnate infamy and name obscene:
    Ah! set thy soaring love on yonder star,
       Thou sin that singest like some holy bird—
It is not so far.

542

O Shiraz City, filled with lovely faces,
    The beauty of the land,
If love you seek, and the Beloved's embraces,
    Just wave your hand.

You will not find a maid fairer or fonder
    Shining on mortal air,
Or wilder bird than that freebooter yonder
    Fall to your snare.

Maiden unspotted, art thou really human?
    Is that an earthly mole?
Never seemed mortal body of a woman
    So like a soul.

2

Burning coal of beauty, break not the broken
    Only one kiss give me—
That is all I ask; would I had not spoken
    My heart to thee.

Pure is the wine, and May, the month of playtime,
    Fills the soft air with song;
No one is certain of another Maytime,
    Not even the young.

There in the garden hear the topers laughing;
    Mark how the wine-jar flows;
A flaming tulip the wine they are quaffing,
    A burning rose.

Love is a mystery past my unwinding,
    Bitter and hard and sore;
Is there no hope a way, HAFIZ, of finding
    To love no more?

HAFIZ, alas! every hair he possesses
    Twines in some wanton's curls;
There's not a hair in all his laureate tresses
    But is some girl's.

564

Bring wine into the garden, on the brink
    cool fountain set the pillows so:
Roses to scatter, and red wine to drink—
    I do not know
If there be more to ask. What dost thou think?

Thus to the nightingale the young rose spake,
    And thus the nightingale made answer meet:
O little rose-tree, tell me for whose sake
    Thou smellest so sweet?
Who from thy bough shall all these blossoms shake?

Walk in the garden, that the cypress may
    Learn from the box-tree of thy perfect grace
In the wind's arms voluptuously to sway;
    O little face,
Why didst thou steal a great man's heart away!

Rosebud-thou art too young to call a rose!—
    I would, while yet the merchants throng to buy.
Thou madest provision, ere thy beauty goes;
    Yea! ere it die
Gather thy pennies, sweetheart—HAFIZ knows!

Hast seen a candle in the way of the wind?
    Beauty is so before the breath of time;
If only thou couldst be a little kind,
    Sweet were this rhyme
As all that musk of China—thy locks untwined.

All birds in the rose-garden of the king
    Come singing—each one hath a different tale
HAFIZ, what song is it that thou dost sing,
    Dread nightingale?
HAFIZ hath nothing but a prayer to bring.

565

Rejoice, my heart, before the springtime goes
    With her fresh laughter;
Soon thou shalt die, and ah! how thick the rose
    Shall blossom after.

Only its roots shall crown thy rotting head,
    While other youngsters
Its petals on the glossy curls shall shed
    Of other songsters;

Thy nostrils with the smell of death be filled—
    They smell the roses;
O be thy attar from each rose distilled
    Before it closes.

Give ear unto the harp, and wisely heed
    What it is saying:
Laugh and be glad; dead thou art dead indeed—
    Make no delaying.

What thou shouldst drink I say not, at whose side
    Thou shouldst be sitting;
Thou art a man of sense, and canst decide
    What is befitting.

Only make haste: each blade of grass you tread,
    Clear for thy reading,
Teaches the myriad lessons of the dead;
    Be not unheeding.

Give not to worldly cares and wasting thought
    Thine hours of pleasure;
The world will take thy all and give thee nought;
    Guard well thy treasure.

Strange is our path and dread; whither it goes
    There is no knowing;
HAFIZ half thinks that the Beloved knows
    Where we are going.

566

Breeze of the morning, at the hour thou knowest,
The way thou knowest, and to her thou knowest,
   Of lovely secrets trusty messenger,
I beg thee carry this despatch for me;
   Command I may not: this is but a prayer
Making appeal unto thy courtesy.

Speak thus, when thou upon my errand goest:
   "My Soul slips from my hand, so weak am I;
Unless thou heal it by the way thou knowest,
   Balm of a certain ruby, I must die."

Say further, sweetheart wind, when thus thou blowest
   "What but thy little girdle of woven gold
   Should the firm centre of my hopes enfold?
Thy legendary waist doth it not hold,
And mystic treasures which thou only knowest?"

Say too: "Thy captive begs that thou bestowest
   The boon of thy swift falchion in his heart;
   As men for water thirst he to depart
By the most speedy way of death thou knowest.

"I beg thee that to no one else thou showest
   These words I send—in such a hidden way
   That none but thou may cipher what I say;
Read them in some safe place as best thou knowest."

When in her heart these words of mine thou sowest
For HAFIZ, speak in any tongue thou knowest;
Turkish and Arabic in love are one—
Love speaks all languages beneath the sun.

570

A thousand ways, beloved, have I sought
   That thou shouldst be my own true love and friend;
Fulfiller of fond hopes—yea! so I thought;
   My answer unto prayer, my journey's end;
   All this and so much more did I intend
      That thou shouldst be.

That thou shouldst come—it was my phantasy—
   One starry night, where we poor lovers dwell,
And all my sorrow with thine own eyes see—
   My vigil share, and make thy bed in hell,
   Know all the torments of my martyrdom,
And learn how long the nights are without thee:
      Then to my heart—my heart I dared to tell—
         That thou shouldst come.

My comrade and my counsellor I said
   That thou shouldst be, the safe abiding-place
Of all the secrets of my heart and head;
   Dear fawn, how all unworthy of the chase
The sun's gazelle himself would seem to me
Wert thou but quarry to my venery!
   Proudly let other queens number their host
   Of beauty-bondsmen, if but I might boast
The imperious regent of my lowly fate
      That thou shouldst be.

Better for HAFIZ had he not been born,
   Unless thou be his comrade and his mate;
He's not the value of a barley-corn
      Unless thou be.

572

My heart in prison is—in Selma's hair;
    Her two thick locks hold it securely bound;
    And day and night, with a most mournful sound,
Cries and laments the wretched prisoner.

O God, take pity on me, whose sad heart
    Is thus deprived of his sweet liberty;
    Selma, vouchsafe me union with thee,
Nor thou too with my enemies take part.

Who says I love not Selma is a liar;
    Who loves not Selma has not Selma seen,
    Else he too in the same sad case had been—
Drowned in the same overwhelming sea of fire.

Selma, my soul I'll place beneath thy heel
    If aught in me hath done my Selma wrong;
    Thine eye sees not, and talks astray thy tongue
Who the like pain as mine can never feel.

Selma, on God alone must I rely;
    Black is the starless night of Selma's hair;
    HAFIZ is lost in the dark windings there:
God be my guide—no other friend have I.

586

Shah, out of heaven came now this sudden song,
   Blazing with jewels as dread Rizwan's throne,
   So fair—I feared to keep it for my own,
Deeming it must to thee, great Shah, belong.

Rippling and bright and soft as Selsebil
   That flows through Paradise his floating hair,
   Sweet-tongued, pure-thoughted, grave yet debonair,
The Spirit of Song unfolded me his will.

Said I: "Why camest thou to such a place,
   Under a roof so very poor as mine?"
   Said he: "I seek another house than thine:
I come to sing before the great Shah's face."

Now is he all awearied of poor me,
   And would within thine august presence stand;
   Great Shah, extend to him thy royal hand,
And call the eager visitant to thee.

591

Song such as this hath need of no man's praise;
    Beauty like this can be concealed from none;
Why should I bold a candle to the rays
        Of such a sun?

Only the pen that out of dewdrops wrought
So new and maidenlike a loveliness,
To clothe the virgin freshness of his thought,
We thank and bless.

Art has no equal to this piece of wit,
    Nor nature on so rare a fancy fell,
Magic or miracle, or maybe it
        Is Gabriel.

True singing still a mystery remains,—
    Never such pearls as these were bored and strung,—
Never the singer of the song explains
        How it was sung.

592

O lion-hearted, ocean-handed King,
    Thou ruler just, sultan, and sovereign,
    Who by thy virtues as thy strength doth reign,
The conqueror of every living thing;

Shah Mesoud, whose reverberating name
    Into all quarters of the earth hath run;
    Wherever blows the wind and shines the sun,
There is thy glory, Mesoud, there thy fame.

Perchance, great Shah, those powers invisible
    That on thy dread intelligence attend
    Even have told thee how thy humble friend
Lately from light to deepest darkness fell.

Yea! by a sudden stroke of skilful Fate,
    The little unpretending three years' hoard
    Out of thy bounty diligently stored
Is stolen: therefore am I desolate.

Last night I had a dream: methought that I
    At morning in the royal stables stood,
    And lo! my mule was munching at his food.
"Thou knowest me?" said he, nosebag awry.

I woke and pondered long. My mule—what might
    That mean? The royal barley—what? O deign,
    All wise Mesoud, omniscient sovereign,
My dream to read—and to fulfil—aright.

596

Conserve of roses is this book of song,
    With dewy tinctures of the violet
Subtly distilled and blent a life-time long,
    With the years sweeter grown and sweeter yet.

It is for this reason that the vulgar kind
    Of singers envious of HAFIZ are;
Their sugar candy is not so refined—
    Mere sticky sweetmeats of the cheap bazaar.

Bitterness fill his mouth for whom my songs
    Are not heard honey to the ravished ear,
And dust upon his head whose malice wrongs
    This limpid verse as running water clear.

How should a man blind from his mothers womb
    Buy with shut eyes a maiden for his bed!
Down the long line of loveliness in bloom
    The sightless dotard all in vain is led.

598

MY little moon, the morning Friday was,
  Of the third month the sixth unhappy day,
When, with a breaking heart, I watched thee fade,
  And thy cheek from my bosom fell away.

The year seven hundred was and sixty-four
  Of the great Prophet's, and thy tender, flight;
Like hail the sudden stroke upon me fell,
  And broke thy gentle blossom in my sight.

Since that dark day the sport of fate I am,
  Of circumstance the idle drifting toy;
Regret is vain—nought else is there to do,
  Since thou art dead, and with thee all my joy.

604

Ismail is dead, of men and cadis best:
His pen, like its great master, takes its rest.

Much wrote he of God's law, and lived it too—
Would I could say as much for me and you!

The middle of the week he went away—
The month of Rajab it was, and the eighth day,

In this uncertain dwelling ill at ease,
To a more ordered house he went for peace.

His home is now with God, and if you write
"The mercy of God," interpreting aright

The mystic letters standing side by side,
You then shall read the year when Ismail died.

605

Kiwam-ed-Din, strong pillar of the state,
Prop of the faith is dead; before his gate
The very sky bowed down—he was so great.

Yet underground he journeys, in despite
Of his unmatched magnificence and might;
From living things he passes out of sight.

With him, too, from this iron world departs
The last protector of the liberal arts;
His day of death is written on our hearts.

The very figures fitly signify
"Learning's last hope"—for so interpret I:
In the eleventh month he came to die.

606

Little sleeper, the Spring is here;
    Tulip and rose are come again,
    Only you in the earth remain,
Sleeping, dear.

Little sleeper, the Spring is here;
    I, like a cloud of April rain,
    Am bending over your grave in vain;
Weeping, dear.

Little flower, the Spring is here;
    What if my tears were not in vain!
    What if they drew you up again,
Little flower!

608

Seese thou this little berry, this green pill?
    It is made of dreams; yet, so sustaining it,
    Thirty fat birds all cooking on a spit
Would not thy belly half so subtly fill.

It is this berry that the Sufis eat
    When they would fall into an ecstasy,
    And tell their precious lies to thee and me;
A little hasheesh is the whole big cheat.

Thirty birds, said I? yea! in one small grain
    A hundred times that number cook for thee;
    Eat thou—it will harm thee not—and thine shall be
Houris unnumbered ere thou wakest again.

613

O you embroidered robe of my young days,
How fast your silken pattern fades and frays;
Saving a dash of colour here and there,
Nothing remains to show me what you were.

Alas! that from Life's pleasant river brink
The water of life must some day surely shrink!
When we like withered rushes all are dead,
And life is an old dried-up river-bed.

It needs must be some day that thou and I
Bid family and friend a last goodbye,
Brother from brother part, and I from thee:
Such, by thy father's dust, is heaven's decree.

Only two little stars up near the pole
May keep together while the ages roll;
Asunder none may rend the Ferkedan—
Shining together since the world began.

Glossary

AAD, according to the Koran, the ancient tribes of Aad and Themoud were destroyed when they ignored the judgment to come.

ABOU ISHAC, or Abu Ishak was the first patron of Hafiz, and was renowned for his debauched lifestyle. He was Governor of Shiraz from 1336 to 1353, when he lost his head, through one of the many changes of dynasty.

ABRAHAM, the patriarch, one of the six prophets of Islam.

ALEPPO, a city in northern Syria.

ANCA, a huge mythical bird, similar to the Phoenix.

ARAK, the poetical name for the dwelling-place of the Beloved, wherever it may be.

ASEF, chief counsellor to Solomon.

BOKHARA, Central Asian city.

EDEN, in Muslim mythology the Fall was due, not to an apple, but to a grain of wheat.

EREBUS, a god of darkness in Greek mythology.

FARS, a province of Persia.

FERHAD, and Shirin are two lovers famous in Persian legend.

GABRIEL, the angel who appeared to Hafiz.

HARUT, and Marut were two angels. They were sent down to earth to experience the temptations of humanity, and fell victim to the beauty of Zuhrah, who learnt from them "the great name of God," and by its power ascended to the planet Venus, with which she became identified in Mohammedan mythology. The fallen angels were punished by being confined head-down in a pit near Babylon, where they were supposed to teach magic and sorcery.

IM'ADDEDIN, Imad Ud-din-Mahamud, vizier of Abu Ishak, and a friend of Hafiz.

ISMAIL, Sheikh Mejdeddin Ismayil, Cadi of Shiraz, died 1355.
JAMSHID, an ancient Persian king who could view the entire world in his magic cup.
KAIKHOSRU, a famous Persian king.
KAIKOBAD , a famous Persian king.
KAWOU, a famous Persian king.
KIWAM-ED-DIN, Aazem Kiwam-ed-daulet-Wed-din, a Grand Vizier of Shiraz, one of the patrons of Hafiz. He died in 1355.
MAGIAN, a Zoroastrian; Magian Elder refers to the tavern-keeper.
MARUT, see Harut.
MESOUD, or Masud, a contemporary ruler.
MENSOUR, Sheikh Mensour was a mystic of Bagdad, who was put to death in 919, on the charge of revealing divine mysteries.
MUSA, Moses.
MUSELLA, or Musalla, a rose garden near Shiraz, which was a favourite spot for Hafiz, and is his burial place.
MUSSULMAN, a Muslim.
NIMROD, a legendary king who tried to burn Abraham to death, but Gabriel turned the fire into roses.
RIZWAN, the gate-keeper of heaven.
RUKNABAD, a stream running through the rose garden of Musella.
SAKI, the cupbearer.
SAMARKAND, the city of Tamerlane, now in Uzbekistan.
SELMA, or Salma, a name for the Beloved in Arabic.
SELSEBIL, a river in Paradise.
SHIRAZ, Hafiz's home city in Persia.
SHIRIN, see Ferhad.
SIDRA, a tree in Paradise.
SIKANDAR, or Iskender, is the Persian name for Alexander the Great, who was fabled to possess a magic mirror, made for him by Aristotle, in which he could see all that was going on in the world, and thus the movements of his enemies.

SOLOMON, the wise king, one of the six prophets of Islam.
SUFI, a member of one of the many esoteric Muslim sects.
THEMOUD, see Aad.
ZUHRAH, Venus. See Harut.

www.ingramcontent.com/pod-product-compliance
Lightning Source LLC
Chambersburg PA
CBHW031249290426
44109CB00012B/495